A DIALOGUE ......
ARNOLD LAZARUS

THERAPEUTICALLY SPEAKING SERIES
Series editor: Windy Dryden

TITLES IN THE SERIES

Published titles

Windy Dryden: *A Dialogue with Albert Ellis*
Windy Dryden: *A Dialogue with Arnold Lazarus*
Windy Dryden: *A Dialogue with John Norcross*

A DIALOGUE WITH ARNOLD LAZARUS

'It Depends'

WINDY DRYDEN

OPEN UNIVERSITY PRESS
Milton Keynes · Philadelphia

Open University Press
Celtic Court
22 Ballmoor
Buckingham
MK18 1XW

and
1900 Frost Road, Suite 101
Bristol, PA 19007, USA

First Published 1991

British Library Cataloguing-in-Publication Data

Dryden, Windy
    A dialogue with Arnold Lazarus: 'It depends'.
    – (Therapeutically speaking)
    I. Title. II. Series
    616.89

    ISBN 0-335-09280-2
    ISBN 0-335-09279-9 (pbk)

Library of Congress Cataloging-in-Publication Data

Dryden, Windy.
    A dialogue with Arnold Lazarus: it depends/Windy Dryden.
        p.   cm. – (Therapeutically speaking series)
    Includes bibliographical references and index.
    ISBN 0-335-09279-9 (pb.) – ISBN 0-335-09280-2 (hb.)
    1. Eclectic psychotherapy. 2. Lazarus, Arnold A. – Interviews.
I. Lazarus, Arnold A.   II. Title.   III. Series.
RC489.E24D78   1991
616.89'14–dc20   91–10807
                                                             CIP

Typeset by Type Study, Scarborough, North Yorkshire
Printed in Great Britain by
J. W. Arrowsmith Limited, Bristol

CONTENTS

PREFACE

The purpose of this series is to explore the ideas of established and emerging leaders in the field of psychotherapy. The interview format was chosen to give the 'feel' of an informal but disciplined discussion of each expert's ideas. It is hoped that the books convey the sense of two colleagues engaged in a searching discussion of the ideas of one of them.

The development of the books followed a standard pattern. Initially, I negotiated with the persons concerned the content of each set of interviews. The experts were given the choice of preparing as much or as little material as they wanted in advance of the interviews. Then the interviews were conducted and transcribed. Finally, both I and the interviewees went over the interviews, tidying up the English, with the latter adding or deleting material as they saw fit. In general, however each book remains faithful to the interviews as they were conducted.

Windy Dryden

INTRODUCTION

Arnold Lazarus was born in Johannesburg, South Africa, on 27 January 1932. He was the youngest of four siblings: when he arrived, his two sisters were 17 and 14 years old, and his brother was almost 9. When he was 5, his second sister gave him piano lessons, and two years later he used to perform in public. 'At age 7 I played the piano like a talented 10 or 12 year old,' he said, 'but when at age 12, I still played like a 10–12 year old it seemed like a good idea to quit.' At age 17 he dropped out of high school with a view to eventually opening a health and training centre as he had become an avid body-builder and weight-lifter ('to overcompensate for the fact that I was a skinny kid who was bullied a lot'). Meanwhile he tried his hand at selling houses, working in large department stores, working for a pharmacist, 'but always allowing lots of time to get to a gym'. By the time Lazarus was 19, he had been persuaded that it would be best to finish high school and go to university. He had shown some talent as a writer, having had stories published in local newspapers in his early teens, and he became the Associate Editor of a South African body-building magazine. When first attending the University of the Witwatersrand in Johannesburg (where he ended up obtaining a BA in Psychology and Sociology in 1955, a BA Honours in Psychology in 1956, an MA in Experimental Psychology in 1957, and a PhD in Clinical Psychology in 1960), he intended majoring in English with a view to journalism as a career, but became intrigued by psychology, 'particularly when I discovered that one could become a psychotherapist without first going to medical school'.

Lazarus spent three months as an intern in 1957 at the Marlborough Day Hospital in St John's Wood in London where he was influenced by the Adlerians at the hospital, especially the Medical Director, Dr Joshua Bierer. He completed his clinical training at Tara Hospital in Johannesburg and then conducted his PhD dissertation with Joseph

Wolpe, MD, as his chairperson. His thesis, 'New group techniques in the treatment of phobic conditions', was the first study to employ systematic desensitization in groups, and it was also perhaps the first time that anyone had devised objective scales for assessing phobic avoidance. For example, acrophobics were required to see how high up they would climb a metal fire escape (no subjects achieved a pre-therapeutic height of more than twenty-five feet). Successfully treated subjects were willing to climb to a height of fifty feet and then peer down for two minutes, eight storeys above street level, and count the number of passing cars. Similar pre- and post-treatment assessments were carried out with claustrophobic subjects.

Arnold Lazarus started a private practice in 1959 when he became registered with the South African Medical and Dental Council as a Clinical Psychologist. By that time he had five professional publications, including one in 1958 where he was the first person to introduce the terms 'behaviour therapy' and 'behaviour therapist' into the scientific literature (*South African Medical Journal* 32: 660–4). After obtaining his doctorate, he served as a part-time lecturer in the Department of Psychiatry at the Medical School in Johannesburg. He became interested in hypnosis and was elected President of the South African Society for Clinical and Experimental Hypnosis. His paper on 'Group therapy of phobic disorders by systematic desensitization', based on his PhD dissertation, was published in 1961 in the *Journal of Abnormal and Social Psycholology*. It caught the eye of Professor Albert Bandura at Stanford University, who invited Lazarus to spend a year in California teaching in the Department of Psychology at Stanford.

Since he had long been unhappy with the political situation in South Africa, he welcomed the opportunity 'to see how the other half lived', and went to the USA with his wife Daphne and their two children, Linda aged 4 and Clifford aged 2. 'It was in many ways an eye-opening experience, but my wife and I were both so homesick that we couldn't wait to return to our extended family members.' But the Lazarus's both grew more and more displeased with apartheid and the overall political situation and within two years they were back in the USA. In 1967 Lazarus became a Full Professor in the Department of Behavioral Science at Temple University Medical School in Philadelphia, where he worked with his former mentor, Joseph Wolpe. It soon became evident that Lazarus had developed views that displeased Wolpe. For example Wolpe was in strong disagreement with Lazarus's emphasis on technical eclecticism, his use of 'cognitive therapy', and his claims that Wolpean behaviour therapy was 'too narrow'. In 1970 Lazarus went to New Haven, Connecticut, as a Visiting Professor and the Director of Clinical Training at Yale University. In 1971 his book *Behavior Therapy and Beyond* was published. This book was referred to in Citation Index as one of the most widely cited works of its kind. It is arguably the first book on 'cognitive-behaviour therapy'. In 1972 the Lazarus family moved to New Jersey and Arnold accepted the rank of Distinguished Professor at Rutgers, the State University of New Jersey. He was aware that Rutgers was founding the Graduate School of Applied and Professional Psychology, which has been an ideal professional environment for him. 'It is an eclectic work-place that fosters stimulating dialogues and debates, and creates a position of open inquiry without any of the personal animosities that were so evident in other settings.'

Among practitioners of psychology, Lazarus is perhaps best known for two major developments: his views on *technical eclecticism* and his development of *multimodal assessment* procedures.

In 1967 he published a short paper in *Psychological Reports* stressing that effective treatment *techniques* may be drawn from many orientations without subscribing to the theories that spawned them. Over the years, and in many different writings, he continued to argue that a clinician who uses only those techniques that belong within his or her preferred theoretical orientation will inevitably overlook effective methods employed by therapists who work from different perspectives. The beguiling idea of combining different theories, he stressed, would only breed confusion. Upon close examination, various theoretical ideas that appear to be compatible usually turn out to rest on totally divergent assumptions. Nevertheless, because techniques may be effective for reasons other than the theories that gave rise to them, there is every reason to eschew 'theoretical eclecticism' and borrow any useful technique from any source – 'technical eclecticism'. Anyone who is familiar with Lazarus's views on the subject will know that his use of technical eclecticism is highly systematic and is not at all atheoretical. He elects to work mainly from within a social and cognitive learning theory perspective because 'its tenets are grounded in research and are open to verification and disproof'. Thus he may employ a technique that was developed within Transactional Analysis, or Gestalt therapy, or existential therapy, without accepting or believing any of the theories espoused by their originators and followers. Lazarus emphasized: 'I have yet to find any effective procedure that cannot be readily explained in terms of social and cognitive learning theory'.

Lazarus's *multimodal assessment* evolved out of his view that too many practitioners embrace unnecessarily delimited and restrictive procedures. Since his first scientific publication in 1956, which called for a broad-spectrum of procedures for treating alcoholics, Lazarus has contended that most treatment approaches are too narrow. He concluded that the more coping skills a client can acquire, the less likely he or she is to relapse. In many writings he has stated:

We are beings who move, feel, sense, imagine, think, and relate to one another. At base we are biochemical/neurophysiological entities. Our personalities are the products of interactive *be*-haviours, *a*ffective processes, *s*ensations, *i*mages, *c*ognitions, *i*nterpersonal relationships, and biological functions (wherein psychotropic *d*rugs are most commonly prescribed). The first letters of these modalities form the acronym BASIC I.D.

In essence, multimodal assessment is the thorough assessment of a person's BASIC I.D. A fundamental premise is that clients are usually troubled by a multitude of specific problems that call for a similar multitude of specific treatments. The multimodal position is that comprehensive treatment calls for the correction of troublesome behaviours, unpleasant feelings, negative sensations, intrusive images, irrational beliefs, stressful relationships, and possible biochemical imbalance. Of course, not every case requires attention to each modality, but according to Lazarus, an assessment or diagnostic process that ignores or glosses over any aspect of a person's BASIC I.D. is likely to be incomplete.

Lazarus's multimodal approach calls for an exact tailoring of the therapeutic climate to fit each client's personal needs and expectancies. It has a strong 'custom-made' emphasis – the form, cadence, and style of therapy are fitted, whenever possible, to each client's perceived requirements. With some, it is counterproductive to offer more than a sympathetic ear; with others, Lazarus asserts, unless therapy is highly structured, active, and directive, significant progress will not ensue. The multimodal assessment, says Lazarus, spells out when to treat family systems rather than individuals, and vice versa. At all times, the question is 'What works, for whom, and under which conditions?'

Arnold Lazarus has been elected President of several professional associations, has served on the editorial boards of twenty scientific journals, has been a consultant to numerous agencies both private and public and has fellowship status in several professional societies. He has received many honours for his contributions, most notably the

Distinguished Service Award from the American Board of Professional Psychology, and the Distinguished Career Achievement Award from the American Board of Medical Psychotherapists. He was also inducted into the National Academies of Practice in Psychology. He is listed in *Who's Who in America* as well as in *Who's Who in the World*. His twelve books and more than 150 journal articles have led him to give invited addresses throughout the USA and abroad. Several opinion polls have cited Arnold Lazarus as one of the most influential psychotherapists of the twentieth century.

1

THEORETICAL PRINCIPLES THAT UNDERPIN THE PRACTICE OF EFFECTIVE THERAPY

WINDY DRYDEN   I would like to start by considering your views on the major theoretical principles that underpin the practice of effective therapy.

ARNOLD LAZARUS   If I may talk about theories in general before answering your specific question, I would like to emphasize that we have to be extraordinarily careful about buying into all our current theories. Extreme caution is required. There are many theories that were considered highly respectable and were touted widely in bygone years that today are viewed with scorn and derision. Perhaps the most obvious is the faculty psychology of Franz Gall and his phrenology that was in vogue about 150 years ago. Many eminent scientists, scholars, physicians and respected thinkers were members of the British Phrenological Society and the American Phrenological Society, replete with learned journals, conventions and congresses. Yet today, phrenology is viewed as a circus sideshow. How many of our current theories might go the same way? My sense is that many of them might be viewed in years to come with the same bemusement, as we regard faculty psychology and bumps on the head today. So if we remember that theories are simply ways of tentatively trying to make sense of the complex stimuli that bombard us, we are going to be in a far better position to advance knowledge.

The theories that I think are the most viable are those that can be refuted. There are many theories in psychology and psychotherapy that seem wonderful, but if you ask the questions, 'How can we test this?' or 'How can we design an experiment, to prove or disprove this theory?', there is no answer. I think those kinds of theories are most unfortunate. For this reason I have favoured social learning theory in a broad sense because much of the evidence comes from laboratory research – it has led to controlled studies. I also like various aspects of cognitive psychology, and I favour material that has come out of the social psychology laboratory. These are the kinds of areas I look toward for the theories that can best explain what happens clinically. Having said that about theories, I want to tie this into how I think people make themselves disturbed, what kinds of principles seem to be operating.

In my opinion there are basically eight separate or interrelated principles. This first is *external stressors*. There are people who undergo traumatic experiences, or incredible pressures are placed upon them, and it is no surprise that these unfortunate people 'breakdown'. In such instances, I don't think that we can say, as some theorists might, 'Well it's all in the mind, it's not the external stressors, it's how they interpret them'. This can be true for less extreme stressors but when it's something catastrophic (for example a man sees his wife and children perish in a fire), you can hardly say that most of the variance is tied into this man's perceptions as opposed to what is actually impinging upon him.

w.d.   Having said that, to what extent do you take into account individual differences to even extreme external stressors? I am thinking about the way people tend to react very differently to the dire external stressor of a concentration camp, for example.

a.l.   You raise the very important aspect of autonomic nervous system stability or lability, the entire genetic diathesis. I think the evidence is rather clear, that people have different thresholds. Some can withstand prodigious amounts of abuse and come through it smiling. So yes, the impact of the external stressor cannot be totally divorced from the biological strength, or weakness of the individual. Those two seem to go hand in hand.

w.d.   What is your second principle?

a.l.   The second principle is something that traditional psychotherapy has made a tremendous amount of: *conflicting or ambivalent feelings or reactions*. In essence, clinically we often meet people who come to us in a tremendous catch-22 situation; they're really undecided, they are torn apart. They have approach–approach conflicts or approach–avoidance conflicts; they are ambivalent and cannot make up their minds. Now clearly their prior learning and experiences have played into this. Nevertheless, this is an important factor in creating disturbance for a lot of individuals. The extreme indecisiveness that so many people manifest needs to be addressed. Many approaches to therapy aim to resolve the conflict and to teach people to take chances, make decisions and break from this inertia that grips them. So I see this as a second important principle.

w.d.   In your experience does this principle reflect itself in particular types of disturbance rather than in others?

a.l.   I think that many disturbances can come from conflicting feelings – anxiety, depression, rage, and obsessive-compulsive disorders are among them. Perhaps some degree of conflict is present in many of the classic neurotic disorders that we see. This, of course, is a standard assumption of psychodynamic theory.

w.d.   What is your third principle?

a.l.   The third is _misinformation_. Here I am simply saying that people will not cope successfully with the demands of life if they don't have necessary information, if they don't know how to respond, how to react in given situations. If they use an incorrect _modus operandi_, they will be hard pressed and will find themselves anxious or depressed or bewildered or back into ambivalence, etc. So to get clear information across to people, I see the therapist's role as that of an educator who will find specific areas of misinformation and actively educate the clients. This is very different from psychodynamic theories and therapies.

w.d.   What are the most common areas of misinformation that you encounter in clients?

a.l.   The most common areas seem to be tied into the perfectionistic demands of our western society, where people believe, for example, that fame and fortune will produce lifelong happiness. So people develop perfectionistic outlooks, they regard themselves as victims of circumstances instead of realizing that their lives are basically controlled by many of their own thoughts and perceptions. They believe that it is good to ventilate anger, and often are into excessive people pleasing. These are some of the common mistakes I see over and over clinically. Others that come immediately to mind are people believing that it is better to live a life where they take no risks, where they play it safe. Many believe that happiness is not their birthright but they have to earn it. The common neurotic believes that if he or she avoids problems and unpleasant situations, these problems and situations will disappear. These kinds of errors, together with dichotomous reasoning, absolutistic thinking and the overgeneralizations that occur are what many clients need to be disabused of.

w.d.   This particular dimension is very much what the cognitive therapies are concerned with.

A.L.   Correct. They address the need to change incorrect assumptions and beliefs about life and living.

W.D.   What is the fourth major way that people in your experience make themselves disturbed?

A.L.   The fourth way, unlike misinformation, is *missing information*. It's not that people have erroneous ideas, but they have failed to acquire adaptive pro-social responses. For example people with clear-cut areas of ignorance, who have skill deficits, and who are simply naive fall into this category (missing information). You meet them clinically and realize that they simply don't know certain essential things that they need to know. For example they display enormous social skill deficits. They have not been taught to develop eye contact, are socially inept, and many do not have a clue as to how to perform in job interviews, how to present themselves in a good light, and how to converse in an appropriate manner.

W.D.   Let's move on to the fifth major way that people make themselves disturbed.

A.L.   The fifth one is *maladaptive habits*. I am thinking here of what can be called conditioned emotional reactions that people acquire through various associations and unfortunate connections of events. This results in complex or just simple habits that people may acquire that get in the way of their happiness. This is different from the four previous examples.

W.D.   Is the major psychological mechanism here that these habits are conditioned?

A.L.   Yes. I think that the major mechanism is that there's an association among events and the association takes place very rapidly, usually involving autonomic reactions, although in the final analysis I think that we human beings will push most things into cognition. However, the sub-cortical learning that takes place in which people form certain associations between events without consciously recognizing this, is what I am alluding to here. I am not thinking of rigid robot-like conditioning. Recent studies strongly suggest that even rats think while they are being conditioned. So I am not talking about a stimulus–response, mechanical conditioning.

W.D.   Clinically what are the major habits that get conditioned, or acquired in this way?

A.L.   A lot of the avoidance habits that people develop where they keep themselves in a vacuum by not doing certain things and thereby create anxiety and depression. Instead of facing their fears and going into the situation, they have the habit of constantly backing away. Simple habits, like nail-biting, or certain compulsive counting rituals that people get into also fall into this category. These problems call for 'habit retraining' rather than 'cognitive restructuring'.

w.d. Since humans 'push these reactions into cognition', you presumably consider that these reactions can be mainly attributed to conditioning factors of one sort or other.

a.l. Correct. That is to say that people develop these reactions without thinking about them. Over time they may realize that when X or Y happens, they typically respond with A and B, where A and B is not an effective response.

w.d. So I am beginning to build up a picture whereby you see some psychological disturbances as being mainly mediated by faulty cognition and other erroneous beliefs, and other major clinical problems which have little to do with that cognitive domain in their acquisition and are mainly to do with some faulty aspect of conditioning.

a.l. That's correct, I think the distinction that you have drawn is a valid one.

w.d. Where do you see the major points of interaction between disturbance that is acquired mainly by cognitive means and disturbance that is acquired by conditioning means?

a.l. It's not discrete. There is an interaction; as many people, most notably Albert Ellis and Aaron Beck and other cognitive therapists, have pointed out, we human beings have a penchant to explain even our basic conditionings cognitively. You can't separate the two. What I am saying is that, if somebody is in a highly stressful situation, for a fairly protracted time period, there are visceral changes and physiological consequences that may be termed an 'autonomic memory'. Certain stimuli come to elicit predictable responses. These responses may be adaptive in one environment but not in another and that's where the problem comes in. In many cases of post-traumatic stress disorder, certain stimuli elicit inappropriate responses. The most common example is that a car backfires and a combat veteran dives for cover.

w.d. Now even though you have discussed some points of inter-action between cognitive factors and conditioning factors, am I right in assuming that in developing a treatment plan it is important for you to know whether a particular maladaptive habit has arisen mainly through misinformation or mainly through conditioning?

a.l. Often yes. It's not always essential for me to know the antecedents, because very often the treatment is one and the same. For example let's say that the person is presenting with phobic reactions and that in one case the phobic reactions were engendered initially because of some misinformation. Meanwhile, this person corrects his or her misconceptions but is still into this conditioned avoidance that I was referring to. Well, exposure is the treatment of choice regardless of the antecedents. But there might be other cases where it is important to know how this arose, because the person might still be embracing misinformation. For example someone believes, 'If I ask a woman out on a date and she rejects me, I will inevitably become deeply depressed'. In such cases, you first want to disabuse them of such faulty cognitions and prove to them that they can make these approach responses, that they are entitled to make these responses, and that there will be no dire consequences. Thereafter you may proceed with your exposure therapy. But with some people you first have to deal with the misinformation if that is what is maintaining the problem.

w.d.   Let's move on to your sixth principle.

a.l.   The sixth has to do with the way that people relate to one another: the undue dependencies, the misplaced affections, the excessive antipathies. Now of course this *interpersonal inquietude* is not a separate principle in the sense of the ones I have previously enunciated, but I think it has to have a place of its own if only because so many people are upset because of loves and hates and dependencies on others. Interpersonal relations occupy in my scheme a very important place. The way we get along with other people, or don't get along with other people, seems to me to be at the very core of our happiness. I would go so far as to say that people who do not have others who love them, care for them, respect them and in turn whom they love, care for and respect are impoverished. However successful, however erudite, however brilliant, talented and charming they may be, these people, will not be happy people. That's why I have included 'interpersonal inquietude' for want of a better term to remind us to address this significant realm.

w.d.   Again from your clinical experience, what have you encountered as being the most frequent aspect of this interpersonal inquietude?

a.l.   It's always hard for me to specify what is most frequent, but certainly one very frequent issue addresses the demands that people place upon one other. So many are hungry for affirmation. They ardently desire significant others to respect them, love them, admire them, reinforce them, and yet they go about it in the wrong way. You see how this ties in with problems related to skill deficits or misinformation. Typically people say: 'It's absolutely imperative that this person responds to me in such a way or it means that the relationship is completely bankrupt.' So what I am saying is that much interpersonal inquietude stems from skill deficits plus demands that people impose on one another.

w.d.   So it's where people try to get affirmation but in a way that is detrimental to the relationships that they are in.

a.l.   Right. The most astonishing thing of all is that highly intelligent people who surely know something that our great-great-grandmothers and ancestors knew (and probably even cavemen and cavewomen knew) namely the cliché that you can catch more flies with honey than vinegar, still seem to overlook this truism. It is strange to have to state the obvious, that if you are not kind, supportive, understanding and loving, you are not going to get the kind of warmth from other people that you desire; that we train other people how to treat us. Individuals who surely know better, respond to significant others in a most ascerbic, critical, attacking and undermining way and then are nonplussed when they find they are not getting the strokes they feel entitled to. I find this quite astonishing, and very frequent in my practice.

w.d.   You were saying that intelligent human beings 'should know better'. However, if you sat them down and asked whether the best way of getting affirmation is through a positive approach to somebody or through a complaining, demanding approach, presumably they would all say 'a positive approach'. How do you account for the fact that in reality people find it so difficult to put that principle into practice?

a.l.   I will tell you what a lot of people have said when I have pinned them down. They have said things like, 'Well, this is how it was in my home' or 'This is how my mother spoke to my father' or 'This is how it was done in our family and this was how I was taught to react'. There is this interesting penchant to leap from one area to another without stopping to think about the consequences of having an abrasive style. If you ask them whether their parents had a close intimate loving relationship, in most cases they say no. Now why wouldn't these intelligent people have concluded on their own that they need to change the way they respond? 'I had no choice, that's how I was taught' is the common answer to such questions. Then there is a common myth: 'In work situations and with strangers, it is important to be on guard, therefore at home I should be able to let down my hair'. Now letting down their hair to some of these people means being downright abusive.

w.d. So you would explain the prevalence of that kind of negative interpersonal style through the principle of modelling on the one hand and a sort of 'let it all hang out' myth on the other hand.

a.l. These two certainly feature prominently.

w.d. Let's move on to your seventh principle.

a.l. My seventh principle brings self-acceptance into the picture. Again this is not intended as something truly separate and discrete, but because so many people come into therapy with unbelievably negative self-concepts, I put down principle number seven as a reminder that a lot of psychological disturbance needs to be looked at as a definite product of *poor self-acceptance*.

w.d. You wrote a paper many years ago called 'Toward an egoless state of being' (Lazarus 1977).

a.l. Right, that was published in the Ellis and Grieger *Handbook of Rational-Emotive Therapy*.

w.d. Do you still hold to that viewpoint, that it's better not to have one attitude to oneself, because we are not just one big 'I', but a myriad of different little 'i's'?

a.l. Yes, and I must point out the term 'self-acceptance' rather than 'self-esteem' is something that I learned from Albert Ellis. My understanding of his view is that if people have high esteem, this places them in a vulnerable position. Let's suppose that you ask someone whether they have high self-esteem and that person says, 'I do'. Then, if you ask upon what they base their esteem, and the person says, 'I am young, attractive, successful and athletic', that's unfortunate because these attributes are temporary. What happens when the person loses some of the youth and agility, will their self-esteem then crumble? So the goal is not to develop self-esteem but self-acceptance which means 'Don't put your ego on the line, accept yourself, your totality, even though there might be lots of little "i's" as part of the big "I", that are less than exemplary.' Despite shortcomings and personal limitations, there can still be self-acceptance.

w.d. Have you encountered the response of clients who say 'That's a good principle but how do you do it?'

a.l. Yes, but not as much as when I have tried to embrace what is called, in some circles, 'an elegant philosophy of life', that transcends what we are talking about, where people aspire to become almost completely non-upsettable. That's when I find most people saying, 'How could one possibly attain that level?'

However, saying to people 'You don't have to feel totally crushed as a person, because you made mistakes in these specific areas, or because you are deficient in these skills' is easier to grasp and there's much less resistance to that idea.

W.D.   Let's look at your final principle.

A.L.   The final one is the basic substrate you might say of *biological dysfunctions*. I am suggesting here that a lot of psychological disturbance is the result of biochemical imbalance. People can come in, very depressed and anxious, or with rigid obsessive-compulsive disorders which have a biological base. You cannot exclude biology. I work in concert with organically oriented psychiatrists who know what drugs to prescribe, while I, the psychologist, do what else is needed in these other seven domains. This tends to facilitate a far better outcome clinically for the person who needs medication. The most obvious examples concerns the treatment of bipolar disorders. The manic-depressive individual often needs lithium carbonate in order to stabilize. My argument is, the person who's only given lithium carbonate without also examining the external stressors in that person's life, the possible conflicts that he or she might have, the misinformation and missing information, that might be present and the maladaptive habits and any interpersonal conflicts that may call for help would be receiving poor therapy. So I developed 'multimodal therapy', which implies that it is necessary to look at each of these areas to make sure that no zone is being neglected.

W.D.   Would you say that there is an implicit philosophy of happy living that underpins your approach to psychotherapy?

A.L.   Yes, the purpose of life, as many experts have pointed out, is to have as much fun and enjoyment as one can, without harming anybody in the process. It is regrettable that there are many people who feel that the purpose of life is to achieve, make a mark, get ahead. If I had the opportunity to treat somebody like Vincent Van Gogh, I myself would not have hesitated to have helped this man be happy, even though this might have deprived the world of great artistic masterpieces. I would have hoped that the man would have lived a long and happy life, and gone to his grave with two ears as it were, and we would have had fewer sunflowers to delight over in our galleries. A question I always ask, when somebody passes away, is, 'Did this person have enough fun on this earth?' as opposed to 'How much money did this person make, or what successes, what achievements, what marks did this person leave on this earth?' If the person has had little fun, I feel it has been a wasted life. I am talking here of course of a long-range hedonism as a guiding philosophy.

w.d. Would it logically follow from what we have discussed about the way people make themselves disturbed that from your viewpoint a happy person is one who doesn't face too many external stressors, has little dominant conflicting or ambivalent feelings, whose attitudes and beliefs are rooted in a clearly based view of the fallibility of human beings and the world, who has little missing information, very few maladaptive habits, interpersonal relationships that are based on healthy interdependency, well-placed affection and little hostility who accepts him or herself to a large degree, and who has been endowed with a biology that doesn't interfere with the successful pursuit of this happiness?

a.l. What you have described would be an extremely effective and happy person, and certainly that's something to hope for. I think that people can have more deficits than the ones you mentioned and still be pretty happy. I think that realistically speaking most people will have all kinds of problems, because I think that life is so complex and human beings have a biological penchant to defeat themselves at times, but that doesn't have to stop them from accepting themselves. I think the fallibility notion that you touched on, and this is a point of course that Ellis has underscored many times, is tremendously important. If people do in fact recognize and fully accept that they are fallible, and that they will never be infallible, they can then strive to be less fallible and feel full self-acceptance.

w.d. From your clinical experience, if you were to point to two major ways of the eight that we have discussed that people get themselves into trouble psychologically, which two would you choose?

a.l. I would have to go for missing information and misinformation, as the two. I don't mean to sound too judgemental here, but the amount of ignorance that pervades the world is a terrifying reality in my mind. I think of everything from drug smuggling to international terrorism, all being very much tied into extreme misinformation and missing information that people have about the sort of values and skills that could make for a happier world. So we are beset by rampant misinformation and missing information all around us. Ignorance is a terrifying reality because people, through ignorance, can do all kinds of horrendous things, so that's why if I were pushed, I would pick those two.

w.d. Now, in reading your book *The Practice of Multimodal*

Therapy (Lazarus 1981 ; 1989) and listening to you here today, one of the things that strikes me, is that you are happy to place the theoretical ideas that we have discussed under the general rubric of social learning theory and you quote Albert Bandura as one of the influential figures there. What interest do you have in taking the concepts that you have outlined and developing a full theoretical statement of your own, rather than relying on somebody else's theoretical framework?

A.L.   I would be interested in doing that if I had the wherewithal. But as I said at the beginning of our discussion, I am aware of the tentative nature of theories and prefer therefore to be somewhat more of an empiricist and to leave the theorizing to others, and to try to understand the frameworks, structures and principles that they have enunciated and see which ones are the best scientifically proven notions that we can draw upon.

W.D.   Finally, what do you consider to be your unique contribution to the theoretical underpinnings of the practice of effective therapy that we have been discussing?

A.L.   I don't know if I have made any unique contribution to the theoretical underpinnings or to any other sphere of our field, but what I have endeavoured to provide is a systematic, comprehensive and effective framework that therapists can use. My objection to most therapies is that they are too narrow. People have a penchant to gravitate to a small range of ideas and strategies with which they are comfortable and they apply this to all-comers even though they claim to do otherwise. What I have tried to provide is a broad-based systematic framework as outlined in my book *The Practice of Multimodal Therapy* that clinicians can use to be far more effective with a wider range of clients.

| 2 |

PRINCIPLES OF
EFFECTIVE THERAPY

WINDY DRYDEN   I want to move on to your views on the practice of
effective therapy. What would you say were the major principles
that for you characterize effective therapy?

ARNOLD LAZARUS   The first principle ties into the rapport that
develops between client and therapist. Some therapists regard this
as the *sine qua non* of therapy, incorrectly so in my opinion. They
view the doctor–patient relationship as the entire healing mechanism. I see the relationship as the soil that enables the techniques to
take root. Nevertheless, in some cases you need nothing more than
a good relationship. There are some people who come for therapy
requiring no more than a good listener, someone who will be
empathic, respectful and attentive. But there are many, many
people who need a lot more than that. They need that special
rapport plus very specific techniques. And if they do not get the
specific techniques, no matter how wonderful the relationship with
the therapist might be, they are most unlikely to show improvement.

Now in a good and effective relationship as I see it, the therapist
will be concise and accurate in his or her speech, he or she will be
perceptive and sensitive to the relevant and highly charged
emotional issues. Effective clinicians also display profound respect
and significant understanding and use humour appropriately.
Most counsellors would probably agree that these are the ingredients of a good client–therapist relationship. There are many studies
showing that facilitative conditions also include empathy, respect,
genuineness, warmth, concreteness, appropriate self-disclosure
and immediacy.

W.D.   One of the concepts that has struck me in your writings, with
respect to the relationship between the therapist and client, is your
concept of the authentic chameleon. Namely that it is important for

the therapist to modify his or her participation in the therapeutic process in order to offer the most appropriate form of treatment for the client being seen as opposed to the situation where the therapist fits the person to the treatment.

A.L. Nearly all therapists tend to pay lip-service to this notion that everybody is unique and you don't want to use procrustean manoeuvres and shove people into preconceived theories, but you want to treat them as individuals. Therapists from diverse schools of persuasion seem to say that. But if you watch what they do, I think that more often than not, they do push people into rather limited and preconceived theories and they use limited methods.

W.D. I would like to focus more on that issue later, but now could you elaborate what you mean by the therapist as authentic chameleon and give some indication of the decision-making principles that you keep in mind when you decide to develop rapport in different ways with different clients?

A.L. Perhaps a good way of answering your question is to start with the negative. The negative in this case is perhaps the way the late Carl Rogers worked. Carl Rogers was certainly not a chameleon. He did not change one iota, as I saw it, from patient to patient or client to client; he was always the same, constantly offering his carefully cultivated warmth, genuineness and empathy to all his clients. The first question one might ask is 'Are there some people who don't respond well to warmth and empathy?' Strange though that may sound, the answer is 'Yes!' There are some people who prefer a somewhat formal, almost austere business-like trans-action. They don't want the therapist to be, in any sense, gooey and supportive. The sensitive perceptive clinician who picks that up and modifies his or her relationship style accordingly will, I think, get further than someone who is loving, warm and huggy with anyone who comes through the door. To be loved and cuddled and hugged is fine for some, but that could be a tremendous turn-off for other individuals.

W.D. You mentioned the loving empathic relationship on the one hand and the more formal business-like relationship on the other. What other dimensions of therapist participation do you think are important?

A.L. As a number of theorists have shown, there are actually two dimensions that co-vary with every client. The two dimensions are supportiveness and directiveness, and I think that therapists need to ask at every moment, how supportive need I be with this person, and how directive?

Howard, Nance and Myers (1987) have discussed this in their book called *Adaptive Counseling and Therapy*. There are four possibilities that come from their conceptualization. The first is high direction and high support. Now a therapist who chooses that combination is very much of a teacher, because teachers direct, instruct and support; good teachers are very supportive and encouraging while being didactic. I think that the most rapid changes occur when clients are ready for high direction and high support.

Now let's take the opposite, which would be low direction and low support. This is the typical psychoanalytic stance, where the psychoanalyst is removed or detached from the scene, says very little, usually sits behind the patient, who is reclining on a couch and does not provide much support or direction. These tactics are part of a continuum. There are times in therapy when a client desires to get things off his or her chest: they simply want to unload. In such cases it would be a mistake for the therapist to be strongly directive or supportive instead of serving as a good listener, at that time. I am saying that I think that the effective therapist switches among and between all of those modes in the chameleon sense.

Let's take another possible combination which is low direction and high support. When one is not directive but quite supportive, the client receives encouragement and affirmation without being told what and what not to do.

Finally, there is high direction, and low support. Here the patient is simply given instructions. For example, someone might be very disturbed and the person is told to go into hospital: 'Right now I am going to call and see if there is a bed, and I want you admitted this afternoon.' That's high direction–low support. I would say that that mode is one that is used least frequently in outpatient counselling and therapy.

w.d.   In terms of your own practice, which quadrant do you find yourself working in most often?

a.l.   I can say without any equivocation: high direction–high support. This is the clinical teaching mode, seeing psychotherapy as an educational process. I think that life-skills training is extremely important. People often come to therapy to learn coping skills in life. There are so many skills that we all need to acquire: occupational skills, sexual skills, interpersonal skills, parenting skills, the list is very long. The more coping skills we acquire, the easier it is to survive in our society. I agree with Gazda and

Goldfried that good psychotherapy is predominantly coping skills training.

w.d.   Coming back to the notion of the therapist as authentic chameleon, how does this concept relate to the therapist moving among the quadrants?

a.l.   It ties into the notion that the person in therapy needs something specific from you, and you ask yourself if you are able to provide the person with what he or she is seeking. Let's say that the person wants some encouragement and advice. Now there are some theorists who say never do that. (By the way 'never' bothers me tremendously. I think it is a serious mistake to overlook individual differences.) This person requires me to be strict, this other person is asking me to be very soft, whereas someone else wants me to be like a drill sergeant, and yet another person wants me to be a caretaker, or perhaps a priest. Now can I fit the particular role, authentically, comfortably, and provide the person with the necessary conditions that will enhance their growth and development in therapy? If my answer is 'No, I can't do that', I ask, is there somebody I know in the community who can. Then I will try to effect an appropriate referral and have done so quite often. Which brings up matching as a very important concept. It is vital to find a really good match between client and therapist.

w.d.   So an effective therapist can offer in an authentic manner different types of relationship, to different clients at different times?

a.l.   Yes, and play different roles.

w.d.   One of the questions that is often asked when I discuss your work with students and colleagues is this. What are the cues that effective therapists identify that lead them to decide to avoid a particular quadrant with a particular client?

a.l.   This may sound naive, but I stand by it. Quite often the therapist simply asks the patient, what kind of relationship he or she would prefer, and one is guided by what the person says. Now I am not so naive as to believe that the patient necessarily knows what is best for him or her, and the therapist might elect somewhere along the line to introduce modifications. However, the more important answer to the question is that one observes the impact any intervention has. So if, for example, I notice with client A that when I am somewhat didactic and directive he or she pushes me away, resists me, seems uncomfortable and moves around a lot, I would change my approach because I am clearly not getting through to the person and it would be a mistake to persist in that mode. I will then shift to a different mode and see what the response is. So in that way, I think of therapy as a heat-seeking missile, you know the way these heat-seeking missiles follow the target and blow it up. Well, we follow the problems. If the problem turns left, we turn left; if it goes down, we go down till we can blow away the problem. This is called 'clinical flexibility'.

I was once watching a therapist who believed very much in self-disclosure, which at times can be very helpful with the right person, but he was disclosing something personal to his patient and the patient was staring out of the window with total disinterest. I was surprised that the therapist had not picked up on that, but he was so intent on his way of doing things, that he continued. Now this would not happen with a good therapist, who would note that the person is bored and is losing attention or is getting a little glassy-eyed. The cues you pick up are fairly obvious most times.

w.d.   Now what clients may want or ask for in terms of a particular type of relationship with a therapist may not necessarily be one that is most therapeutic for them. From what you said earlier you seem to go along with that, although you did mention that most often what clients want or ask for is therapeutic. Apart from obvious cases where clients seek a relationship with you that is unethical, what instances are there when you would not seek to meet clients' preferences for a particular type of therapeutic relationship?

a.l.   Where the literature has shown that specific techniques are called for, and the patient wants pure insight because this is what the person thinks therapy is all about. When the person says, in essence, 'I don't want to do the things that you say will overcome my problems; I want to talk about my childhood, I want to examine my dreams and I want you simply to listen, reflect and interpret.' It is often difficult to dissuade them. Let's say that this person is obsessive–compulsive or is very depressed; I would be inclined to think that pure insight therapy is a waste of time (because that's what the literature suggests). Now what I may do is try to 'bridge' by going along with the person, following their wishes while enhancing our rapport. Then I would gradually shift them over into other things that would be more productive.

w.d.   Let's move on to your second principle of effective therapy.

a.l.   These are not in order of importance. The second one that comes to mind is the need for a thorough assessment, by which I mean that you cannot overstate the value of examining exactly who and precisely what you are dealing with, so that you can select appropriate interventions, and develop the most facilitative relationship and place everything in a proper context. Most of the field is tri-modal; they talk about *ABC* (affect, behaviour and cognition) and would claim that a thorough and adequate diagnosis or assessment involves those three modalities – *ABC*. I have contended that it is important to separate mental imagery from cognition. I have noticed that many therapists who talk about affect, behaviour and cognition will gloss over imagery. And yet imagery is such a powerful central guiding modality that I see it as pivotal. A careful examination of a person's mental imagery tends to yield penetrating insights into understanding how a person perceives him or herself in the world. In addition to establishing what the person's thoughts are, we also need to know the pictures that go along with those thoughts. Consequently I attend to *C* for cognition, and also check into *I* for imagery. I try to determine the pictures and the associated images that go along with specific thoughts, values, attitudes and beliefs.

Next, sensations must be separated from emotions or affects. Thus, when somebody is thinking something or picturing something, I want to know what sensations the person has. It can be argued, unless you believe in extrasensory perception, that everything we know is due to something we have seen, smelt, heard, tasted, or felt. To ignore our basic five senses is to overlook something that is very important in understanding a person, because people are very much attuned to the pains and pleasures of life, as conveyed through their bodies. When giving homework assignments, if someone tells you what great joy he or she gets from music, you can make recommendations accordingly. If people gloss over these things, they miss vital information. So I am saying in addition to affect, behaviour, cognition (*ABC*) let us add two more dimensions – imagery and sensation.

Moreover, behaviour not only is concerned with intra-individual reactions but *includes interpersonal responses*. So let's not bypass interpersonal processes. Let us not forget to consider what people want from other people, what they give to other people and how rich or poor they are interpersonally, what their demands and expectations are *vis-à-vis* others.

The final modality I want to mention is the biological substrate. The *ABC* misses out on the fact that there is a neurochemical, psychophysiological substrate to everything. Clinically it is important to ask about diet, nutrition and health habits, in addition to the use of recreational and prescribed drugs. What I have been trying to spell out is what I regard as the framework for a thorough assessment.

w.d.   Right, and this has given rise to the acronym BASIC I.D., where *B* stands for behaviour, *A* for affect, *S* for sensation, *I* for imagery and *C* for cognition (BASIC); then we have *I*. which stands for the interpersonal factors and D. for drugs/biology.

a.l.   Right. This framework is intended to remind practitioners to address each interactive dimension.

w.d.   Now I teach a course on theories of psychopathology and recently some students have said: 'OK, that sounds comprehensive, but what Lazarus has neglected is the whole realm of spirituality'. How would you answer this particular criticism?

a.l.   To bring in spirituality as a separate modality strikes me as a mistake. When people talk about a spiritual, transcendental uplifting peak experience, what are they really referring to? As I see it, they are talking about an experience in which there is a powerful belief combined with equally strong feelings, added to vivid imagery and compelling sensations. People tend to label this as a 'spiritual' experience. Now we know we can add angels and God and all kinds of other constructs to the BASIC I.D. but in science, of course, parsimony is paramount. You try not to add explanatory constructs unless they are absolutely essential. So I agree that people can have experiences that go beyond pure emotion, into something that could be called 'spiritual', but I would explain it as I just have by the powerful and synergistic interaction of these other modalities.

w.d.   If another multimodal therapist who was more spiritually and religiously inclined than you wanted to add a spiritual modality to the BASIC I.D., how would you respond?

a.l.   I would wonder what specific experiences they would be discussing under that spiritual heading. If there was a mystical overtone to it, I would not be pleased because I see little value in mysticism and I would therefore not look upon this with great favour. But if they were talking about very strong beliefs plus powerful reactions that seem to go beyond purely emotional and sensory inputs and they wanted to call that spiritual, I would say 'Be my guest'.

w.d.   In terms of the BASIC I.D. where it is important to assess across those modalities, do you undertake a thorough assessment with every client before implementing treatment strategies and techniques?

A.L.   With some people, their main problems are quite obvious and it is unnecessary to traverse the entire BASIC I.D. I am strongly opposed to rigid rules that apply across the board. Speak to any student who has been through multimodal training with me and ask him or her how I answer any general question. You will be told that I usually say: 'It depends'. I am wary of any dogmatic sequencing in therapy. I constantly stress the notion of individuality and uniqueness. So indeed with some people, in the first minute of the first session it might be expedient to zero in with a technique, administer a specific procedure, hand out advice or what have you; with others that would be anathema. These kinds of determinations can be made rather quickly. This is a major reason in my opinion why other approaches to therapy are very popular. They give the therapist a false sense of security by prescribing and proscribing very specific actions. If somebody says, I never do this or I never do that, they don't have to think for themselves.

I am advocating a much more frightening way of proceeding where clinicians have to think for themselves. They must often make split-second decisions. So getting back to your main question let me repeat that I do not carry out a thorough BASIC I.D. assessment with everyone who walks through the door, because quite often it is not necessary. During the initial interview, you obtain relevant antecedents, examine ongoing behaviours, explore the consequences of the client's actions, and look for the interpersonal context. Some clients have two or three circumscribed problems and if these are properly addressed, it can make a big difference to their lives. However, if while working with the person, you run into road-blocks, dead-ends, it is time to start bringing out the heavy artillery as it were, the big guns, and start doing a thorough BASIC I.D. assessment to see what may have been missed in this case. More often than not, this does tend to shed light on the problem and we can go on from there.

W.D.   Also on the issue of assessment, you once said to me that multimodal therapy is *not* a distinct school of therapy. Rather yours is an approach which flows from multimodal assessment.

A.L.   Correct.

W.D.   And yet you accept invitations to write on multimodal *therapy*. You've written books containing that particular title. I wonder if you could help me to understand this apparent discrepancy.

A.L.   I have argued that clients' needs are often better served when

they are treated in a multimodal rather than say a unimodal or
bimodal fashion. But you are right, there is no such thing as
multimodal *therapy*. Because when using desensitization, assertiveness training, cognitive disputation, or shame-attacking exercises, the multimodal therapist has selected a strategy that seems
appropriate at this moment for this particular client. But these are
not exclusive multimodal therapy techniques. Rather, a multimodal clinician applies the strategy that seems best suited. So there is
no specific therapy that can be called multimodal therapy, but
there is a way of working therapeutically, in a multimodal fashion.
This is a most significant point.

w.d. But aren't you in a sense implying, by calling your therapy
'multimodal therapy' and allowing it to appear that way in print,
that there is such a thing as multimodal therapy?

a.l. I don't think it's terribly misleading, because one is then
working in a multimodal fashion. Perhaps one ought to call it
multimodal assessment followed by *appropriate therapy*, or something of that kind. How about saying that multimodal assessment
enhances the broadest and most apposite strategies and leaving it at
that?

w.d. OK, what is your third principle of effective therapy?

a.l. The third is a combination of technique selection and adherence or compliance. I am suggesting here, as I have said before,
that there *are* specific treatments of choice, that we have reached a
position of being able to prescribe specific therapies for certain
problems and that if therapists are not aware of, or not skilled in,
the appropriate techniques, they are most unlikely to remedy
certain conditions. For example let's say that you have a woman
with vaginismus, which is a condition that produces a contraction
of the vagina so that penetration becomes impossible. Now sex
therapists have shown that very specific methods are effective in
the treatment of vaginismus, which consist of having the person
relax and then progressively inserting various different-sized
dilators under conditions of relaxation. The mechanical dilation
may be enhanced by using imagery involving more and more
intimate sexual associations.

When treating phobias, as far back as 1919, even Freud said it
was necessary to have people expose themselves to the feared
situations. So the technique of choice with phobias is some form of
exposure. People who have compulsions and rituals need to be
taught response prevention where the therapist actually shows
them how to prevent themselves from carrying out the ritual.

There are many specific treatments of choice for many conditions. In the treatment of bulimia, the work of many researchers has shown that these people do not respond to a traditional insight-oriented approach or person-centred therapy, but they require a much more disciplined training programme focused on their eating habits. Teaching them to eat three meals a day, using, in some cases, response prevention when these people want to purge (i.e. you prevent them from purging) is often effective. Clinicians must be *au fait* with the strategies that have been proven effective.

w.D.   You have often said that it is important to choose techniques from a wide variety of sources without buying into the theoretical ideas that have spawned the therapeutic approaches in which these techniques are used. But on reading your writings it does seem to me that in a way, most of the techniques that you use do stem from traditional cognitive-behaviour therapy. Would you agree with that?

A.L.   Yes, I agree to some extent. The reason for that is that those are the techniques that seem to have been shown to be the most effective for restoring function in most people. I have people in therapy where I don't use cognitive-behaviour therapy techniques, people who come to me because what they are looking for is a better appreciation of who they are and what they are about. Here my treatment trajectory is quite different. In these cases the therapy is less technical. Sometimes we are purely two lost souls trying to find some meaning in a cosmos of infinite complexity.

I also use techniques that cognitive-behaviour therapists have tended to frown upon. For example I draw on the empty chair technique, from Gestalt therapy and psychodrama, explaining it in social learning theory terms as a variant of role-playing and I also use an imagery technique in which people go back in a time machine to confront their adversaries in the past. Let's say that somebody is 30 years old and they go in a time machine back to when they were 10, and they speak to themselves at age 10 even though they are now three times as old and comfort themselves. I explain this as desensitization whereby the person overcomes lots of sensitivities by reliving some of these experiences in a different context. So you see how I tend to explain what I do in a social learning theory framework but will draw on several techniques outside of the cognitive-behaviour therapy realm.

w.D.   Following on from that, what for you is the relationship between technique selection and treatment effectiveness as determined by research?

A.L. To a large extent the first requirement of technique selection is to be able to determine whether there are data to suggest that this kind of a technique is the method of choice. So being aware of the research outcome literature is important for the practising clinician who will use that as a very important guiding principle. But because people are unique and different, one has to often fly by the seat of one's pants to invent things on the spur of the moment, and draw upon methods that are less than immaculately researched, and quite often develop principles of one's own in the consulting room.

W.D. What you are saying then is that in the first instance particularly where research seems to indicate the application of certain therapy techniques, you start off by using these well-established techniques. What happens then if the predicted therapeutic improvement doesn't occur?

A.L. This is very often when I start bringing out the thorough, complete, systematic multimodal assessment for examining what have I missed in the BASIC I.D. I look for subtle or not so subtle interactions that I have glossed over. In concert with the client, I try to work out what has gone wrong, why this is not going according to plan, and what this unique individual may require from me.

W.D. Is it here that you use techniques that are less well-documented in terms of research?

A.L. Two things may happen. The assessment may show that I am somewhat off base, and as a result I may draw on the other well-researched procedures. On the other hand it may show that this client and I have got to invent something that will be acceptable to this person, in which case we go off the beaten track.

W.D. On the one hand you advocate a scientifically based practice of psychotherapy and yet on the other hand, you are prepared to enter a therapeutic realm where researchers have not yet trodden. For example I believe you sometimes use techniques from neuro-linguistic programming, where research has not demonstrated that such procedures are effective. When you go off the beaten track, as it were, does it lead to any conflict for you?

A.L. It does not lead to conflict and I want to give you some fairly clear examples of how that operates. I was working with a young lady who had developed a cat phobia after watching some horrendous cable television programme, in which feline monsters who were possessed by the devil had attacked and gouged out the eyes of a number of people, who all came to a grisly end. Whether or not this was a sufficient explanation for this young woman's subsequent terror of cats is not the point. Initially I used a desensitization format with her, the standard well-researched laboratory-based desensitization, which consisted of having her deeply relaxed, while visualizing cats in the distance getting closer and closer, and so on. It did not work. So I remembered a technique drawn from neurolinguistic programming (NLP). Now while I consider NLP to be theoretically unsound, and scientifically untenable, one of the NLP techniques consists of imagining the phobic object and shrinking it down in size to a tiny little ant which you can then crush or stomp on. Now their overall scientific rationale is not acceptable, but as a technical eclectic, having heard about this *procedure*, I decided to borrow the technique since the 'tried and true' desensitization had failed. In this case, the pseudo-scientific method worked. That is to say the shrinking of the cats in her imagination, making them smaller and smaller, over and over, followed by some *in vivo* desensitization in which she exposed herself to some friends' cats in actuality, did the trick. Now was I troubled when saying to her 'Why don't you now try shrinking the cats down and see what happens?' The answer is no, I was not troubled. How do I explain it? Not according to NLP theory, but again in a social learning theory framework one can talk about self-efficacy, self-control and desensitization. You don't have to draw upon NLP theory just because it is an NLP technique.

I have in my hand a letter that arrived yesterday, and it is rather useful to draw upon this example. Here was a man who suffered from hyperventilation and attendant anxieties. He saw quite a few therapists who had done state of the art and science procedures that had not worked with him. When he came to me I followed in their footsteps and tried the usual things you do with hyperventilation, from teaching him rhythmic breathing to dealing with some of the anxieties using desensitization, assertiveness training and other mainstream methods. But the man complained that he was not free from hyperventilation for a day. Not even one good day had been achieved. At best he would have a few hours of freedom and then he would feel himself hyperventilating with attendant light-headedness, dizziness and all kinds of palpitations and problems. He had consulted an expert on the subject who again went into special diaphragmatic breathing. I might say that he had seen many other therapists who had looked into his family dynamics and his intrapsychic dynamics, but nothing seemed to be helping this fellow. Then in one session I happened to make a chance remark.

He was complaining about being infantile and I said to him something like, 'Well, all of us I guess have a child in us'. And he seemed to sit up and take great notice at that silly retort of mine. So I thought of transactional analysis that talks about parent, adult and child ego states; again, an approach that theoretically I am at odds with. But why not draw upon their parent–adult–child conceptualization if it is going to make sense to this man? So I began to explain transactional analysis and how he could choose to get into the child ego, the frightened child, the happy child, the adult, the parent and this man gobbled that up with glee. Again for whatever reasons I was talking his language. And so what I did with him was to emphasize that while hyperventilating, the frightened child was taking control. So when this occurred he was advised to say to himself 'I am in my frightened child state and I must find a way of slipping into the adult mode'. Now this sounds rather trite. However, he reported to me at the next session that he had had more free (asymptomatic) days than ever before in the past ten years. So I extended this idea I amplified on the frightened child and we used imagery that involved talking to the frightened child and getting into the adult mode and so forth. Then he wrote me a letter and asked a few questions and said how this was working and I wrote back and told him a few more things about getting into the frightened child, and getting out of the frightened child. I want to read the opening sentence from his letter that just arrived in yesterday's mail.

'Dear Arnold: Things have improved greatly with me since your letter of 31st July. My hyperventilation has been easily controlled, in fact all of August and September thus far have found me almost completely without symptoms.' The remainder of the letter elaborates on how wonderful that is.

Look what I did. I went out of cognitive-behaviour therapy, talked about transactional analysis and gave him ideas that are not well researched in laboratory circles and yet the result was salubrious. That's another case in point.

w.d.   So the way you have described the matter here, technique selection is not a mechanical process.

a.l.   It's not at all mechanical. It's all very well to know that somebody is likely to respond to *in vivo* desensitization, or shame-attacking exercises, or response prevention. But implementing that is an art. You have to accommodate the technique to the idiosyncratic properties of each individual so that client and therapist form a liaison that can promote adherence or compliance.

Compliance is one of the biggest problems that all clinicians face. We can have our answers at our fingertips and know exactly what the client needs to do, and recommend it, but how are we going to get this person to comply? That's where the art form comes in. This is a point I have tried to cover in my book *The Practice of Multimodal Therapy* (Lazarus 1981; 1989) that psychotherapy is both a science and an art and as an art this is where you use the relationship in a special way to try and see to it that the person will comply.

This is often where paradoxical procedures are quite useful. When people are noncompliant, for example, I might say 'Well, I am quite sure that you probably won't carry out this assignment so I am not going to be disappointed when you come to the next session and tell me that you didn't do it'. That sort of a meta-communication will often get the person to come back and say 'Guess what, I did do it!' I remember one time giving a homework assignment to somebody and the person hadn't carried it out and I said somewhat paradoxically: 'I am terribly sorry but I had overestimated your strengths, and had given you something to do that was much too demanding, so we can water it down accordingly'. And the person said 'No, no, it's not that at all, it was just that I didn't have the time'. When I said that I had overestimated his strengths, that got to him. These are just some of the nuances of the art of getting people to comply. So technique selection is not mechanical and its implementation is an art form.

w.d.   And presumably the use of such paradoxical communications has to be firmly based on the knowledge that you have of your client and predicting the likely response that he or she may have to such techniques?

a.l.   Correct, you have to be sure that you know this person well enough to know that if you say *A* and *B* to him or her, *C* and *D* will result, and that *C* and *D* will be positive, because with somebody else it could backfire completely.

w.d.   What is your fourth principle of effective therapy?

a.l.   The fourth principle could be 'Know your own limitations, and other clinicians' strengths'. This is especially applicable to people like myself who work in areas where there are many therapists. It is obvious that clinicians who work in rural areas, and are the only therapists within a radius of 150 miles, don't have the luxury of being able to refer clients to the most appropriate resource. Nevertheless, most of us are not in that situation, and I think it is incumbent upon clinicians to know who and what is available in their area, so that one can make an appropriate referral. Now sometimes the referral is not to another therapist, it might be to a group like Alcoholics Anonymous, Overeaters Anonymous, or Parents without Partners. In this country [USA] we have many other self-help groups that one can refer people to. I have at times referred people to fashion consultants, financial advisers, accountants, lawyers to deal with certain situations that they have brought up in therapy.

However, the most pertinent referrals are to colleagues who I think have skills that I do not possess or have personal qualities that I do not have, that in my judgement will blend much better with this individual. Clearly if one is going to effect this referral it needs to be done fairly soon. Once people have established a bond with you they might be very hesitant to go to somebody else, even though the other person would be better for them. But usually in the first session, I am able to tell whether or not in my opinion there is a good match and whether or not I think that I can be helpful to this person, and if the answer is, I cannot, I try to think of who might. In these instances sometimes the referral is obvious, they need somebody of a different skin colour, somebody who speaks Spanish, somebody of a different sex, and so the referral is tailor-made in that sense, but at other times it is far more subtle. For example perhaps they need somebody who has a way with certain words.

There is another point here that needs to be underscored. I have a colleague who I think is absolutely wrong theoretically, because he subscribes to unproven theories about biofeedback. He has elaborate machines with flashing lights that are very impressive. Recently I was working with one client who seemed ideal for this type of thing. I suspected that this person would like the glitter; it would be like sending her to Las Vegas as it were. And I was right. She responded wonderfully to the biofeedback and thereby reinforced my colleague's false beliefs, whereas I would argue that it was not biofeedback *per se* that proved effective, but the placebo and suggestion.

These are examples of what I referred to as knowing your limitations. Now limitations that involve poor or incorrect client–therapist matching will surface early in the therapy. Later on in some cases, a different process may emerge. You are working with somebody and the person remains depressed and anxious, upset, conflicted and tormented in spite of your best attempts. You double-check your assessments and you just don't have an answer.

This is where I would now want a second opinion; somebody might spot something that I had missed. And I would tell the client, 'I think we need a second opinion here, I am missing something; I have a high regard for my colleague so and so, and would recommend that you see him or her'. Most people will comply, and indeed it has happened that this other person has been able to put his or her finger on something I have missed, just as I have done for them at times when they have referred people to me. We can't be all things to all people. So this principle of knowing one's limitations and other clinicians' strengths is a very important one, and referral to me is a very important technique if you will.

w.d.   What do you think are your own personal lacunae and limitations as a therapist?

a.l.   Well, I suppose the main limitations have to do with client categories. I am not especially good with seriously disturbed people; I think that we need expertise, and special training to be really good at dealing with schizophrenics, for example. You have to work with schizophrenics a good deal and, for whatever reason, be motivated to deal with that population. My experience with that population is limited. I am not very good when it comes to substance abuse, drug addicts etc., again for similar reasons. So when people come to me and I make this kind of diagnosis I ferret out people in the community who are expert in these areas.

I am not especially gifted in working with adolescents. I see some of them in a family context, but there are other clinicians who are really wonderful at reaching adolescents, they can speak their language and they are up on the latest rock bands or whatever it takes to establish the rapport that I lack. I don't do well with child abusers because I have a basic abhorrence and would refer them out. So you see there are these gaps in my repertoire, but there are people in this community who can step in. Some are very well trained in eating disorders so if someone is anorexic or has bulimia nervosa I know to whom to refer this person.

You might ask well what is there left for me, and the answer that I would come up with is, I do very well with people who have stress-related problems, anxieties, tensions, depressions, phobias, compulsions, marital problems, sexual problems, and a variety of interpersonal conflicts and deficits. I seem to have a talent for helping clients cope with difficult people. So there is a fair amount still left for me to work with.

| 3

PROBLEMS AND DIFFICULTIES IN CLINICAL PRACTICE

WINDY DRYDEN   I would like now to discuss the problems and difficulties that you experience in the practice of psychotherapy.

ARNOLD LAZARUS   Allow me to preface this by saying that I think that most problems and difficulties stem from the fact that we don't have a really thorough and penetrating assessment repertòire. Most times when we run into problems and difficulties I submit it is because we really don't understand what we are doing, who we are working with exactly, and so we make blunders, we miss the point, we bypass important cues and then therapy falters or grinds to a halt. So if we had a way of really magnifying or refining our assessment protocols and making them far more compelling, I think we would have fewer problems. I can't stress enough that I believe that inadequate assessment produces most of the problems, and the complexity of human beings makes it very hard for us to know when we really have made an accurate appraisal of an individual, a couple, a family or a group.

Having said that, one of the main problems that we have already touched on is the issue of compliance. Let's assume that we have made a sufficiently accurate assessment to be on target regarding what probably will be best for this person, that we have been able to tune into the style, the cadence, the atmosphere that this person will respond to. Now the issue that we face is how do we get this person to carry out responses that will make a difference in his or her life. Notice what is being implied here is that if we can get people to do things differently and to do different things (the *doing* is important) significant change will then occur. I think it is not enough if people just think, they need also to take action, and that's what I regard effective therapy as being geared towards – effective action-taking. Prochaska and DiClemente (1986) have said that some people come into therapy in a precontemplative phase, others are contemplative and others are action oriented. If somebody is precontemplative, this poses a tremendous problem in terms of getting anything accomplished, because often these people don't even know if they want to be there, if they should be there, and there is a good deal of skill required to get them into the contemplative stage where people can consider, think through things differently, and examine their options. It is in the action stage, where they can do things differently.

Some of the problems have to do with the client's state of readiness which is another concept that Howard, Nance and Myers (1987) have written about which ties into Prochaska and Di-Clemente's (1986) ideas of these stages of development. So one has to ask, 'How ready is the person for change?' Problems arise when one has not made an accurate assessment of readiness, when one thinks that somebody is open to action whereas in fact they block you off because they are nowhere near that phase in their own development. So in a global sense I think that a lot of problems stem from some of these issues.

The other aspect I would like to mention is that therapists rely very much on selective information. We see our clients within the confines of our offices; it is rare that we pay home visits or get a chance to see them operating under natural or social conditions. We rely almost exclusively on oral self-reports and what we can infer from our observations. We make some far-reaching inferences which are often incorrect. So problems and difficulties arise from that. I should add that there are therapists who I think make a very big mistake. They consider it unnecessary to see people outside of the office, because they consider that what goes on in the consulting room is a true microcosm of what will go on in other relationships. So that the way the client responds to you will be typical of the way the client responds to other authority figures or significant others. I strongly disagree with that and believe that many, many events are situation specific and person specific, that the client may respond one way to you and react quite differently to others. There may be degrees of overlap and there are commonalities, but I think that it is a mistake to say that what goes on in the consulting room is an accurate reflection of what goes on with all other relationships.

W.D.   So, tying this into what we were discussing earlier, are you saying that most of the problems and difficulties you experience are due to missing information?

A.L.   Yes, missing information, the inability to really know where we are heading in many instances.

w.d. So are you saying that if only you had that missing information, then everything would turn out well?

a.l. I believe if we had that additional information we could certainly be in a better position to apply the correct methods in the most appropriate ways and that we would predict and control the outcomes far more effectively. I think it is good to cite a case in point to illustrate these general principles.

In working with a married couple, what struck me in a number of sessions was that the wife was rather vituperative, somewhat hysterical and that the husband was very sensitive to these high decibel outbursts. When his wife hit him with a barrage he put up a shield and communication would stop. Then he would often withdraw further and further. I picked up that interaction and advised the wife to be very careful in the style that she employed with her husband, and that he in turn might be well advised to catch himself while withdrawing in order at least to have dialogue and not run away from the scene. After this dual intervention I thought we might make some headway. We didn't. It didn't change anything, and as I got to know the couple better I saw why. I now understood something that was not clear in the first few sessions. Namely that the husband was an incredibly hypersensitive individual, who even if his wife spoke to him in a manner that you or I might consider supportive or understanding or non-critical, it would still strike him as critical. This was not apparent to me initially and so it called for very specific attention. Moreover, the main bone of contention was that the wife wanted to have a child, because she thought that time was running out biologically for her. The husband felt ambivalent about having children and argued that he didn't want to bring a child into the marriage until it was functioning on a higher plane. This was an inordinate and enormous clash point. These things were not evident to me when I applied my first intervention or I would have realized that it would be for naught, because we were missing some of the more important interactions. So that's a fairly obvious and simple case in point, and I come back to saying that a lot of times our problems emanate from insufficient understanding of who and what we are dealing with.

w.d. Apart from missing information, what other problems and difficulties do you experience with clients?

a.l. Who are the most problematic clients? Obviously the very disturbed, the deeply depressed, the encrusted obsessives, are difficult for anybody, so there is no point in dwelling on the obvious. Let's talk of somewhat more subtle problems that one runs into. I am thinking of people who seem to be functioning fairly adequately, but who are inordinately dependent and extremely confused about issues. A case in point is a woman who calls me regularly two or three times a week, between sessions, and the messages are pretty much 'I don't know how I am going to get through today. I don't know what I am going to do about my daughter, my son, my husband. When I am at A I want to be at B, when I am at B I want to be at C and when I am at W, I want to be at Q and R. How do I walk? How do I put one foot in front of the other?' Any advice, support, or understanding that is offered gets 'Yes but', which means the person has just defeated whatever you were saying and one emerges from encounters with people like that feeling quite inadequate as a therapist.

There are other people that remind me of custard pies. Imagine trying to nail a custard pie to a wall. You pick up this gooey pie and you push in the nails and the goo just runs everywhere, there is no substance. There are such people, and often they are labelled borderline or narcissistic personalities by some clinicians. I don't think that the labels do much, but there are some people where there is no substance, you cannot get a grip on anything. You push in one direction and it pops out in another and you just feel yourself covered in goo and then the goo runs into your eyes so that you are blinded. Quite often this is the feeling that emerges after sessions with people of that kind.

w.d.   I think most of us would find working with such people problematic and difficult, but is there something about your own interactive style, your own preferences for being with people for example, that makes working with such individuals particularly difficult?

a.l.   In discussing this with some of my colleagues who don't mind working with such people, I've noted that their expectations are different, they don't expect the people to change and are not put out by the fact that they keep on going round in circles. I think that it is my nature to want to see progress and movement and when I don't see people benefiting, I feel frustrated, so it's quite likely that I take more responsibility than some of my colleagues who don't feel put out by what I have described. So I think that might be one process in me.

w.d.   OK, so knowing that you have what psychoanalytic therapists disparagingly call excess therapeutic zeal, does that mean that you refer such people elsewhere because you consider that you might not be the best person to help these people?

A.L.   The answer, I think basically, is yes. I often ask clients, 'How long do you think therapy should last?' Some say, 'I think no more than ten meetings would be in order'. I had a woman who said 'Well, I think that three or four years of weekly meetings ought to be set aside'. I immediately referred her to a psychoanalytically oriented therapist who is somewhat geared to that pace whereas I would find it quite unreinforcing to work with somebody in that fashion. So that was a clear case in point.

W.D.   So, do you tend not to work with people who are severely disturbed?

A.L.   As I had said earlier, my experience with chronic psychotics, schizophrenics, substance abusers, character disorders, psychopathic personality types is very limited. My client population is drawn from a different level of functioning. Many of the people that I see are in fact professionals who are coping and functioning, but are having serious or semi-serious problems in other areas. So I would say that personally speaking I am not an expert when it comes to the seriously emotionally or mentally disturbed individuals. I might add, however, that there are people whom I have trained, who work wonderfully with that population. There are some people who are marvellous with geriatric clients, they have just got a way with older people, and others are marvellous with adolescents. I work best generally with adult patients.

W.D.   Adult patients who don't require therapy lasting for a period of years?

A.L.   Generally yes, although if you take a look at my client load, you would find that I have some people who have in fact been seen for a number of years, who have made slow, but steady progress in those instances.

W.D.   Do you find that work frustrating, since as we said before you like to see progress?

A.L.   Truthfully yes. I have one lady whom I have seen now for four years, and she will come to a session and bring up the same issues that we went over two years ago. It's as if that never happened; we have to start again. One hangs in. Clearly it didn't penetrate the last ten times, so let's see if we can make it stick this time. But there is a certain sense of frustration. We have been over that time and again. Why hasn't it sunk in? Where am I going wrong?

W.D.   In such cases do you assume most of the responsibility if clients don't change?

A.L.   Most but not all. I think that it is reciprocal, but certainly there are those that place the onus entirely on the patient, saying that if the person is not getting better it is because he or she is resisting or doesn't want to get better. I find that line of reasoning unacceptable. I say that if they are not getting better it is probably because I haven't found the appropriate way to enable or empower them to change. Perhaps there is some vested interest they may have in not responding or there may be saboteurs in their family, who are undermining the progress. Those are the kinds of thoughts that come to mind.

w.d.   Are there any other problems or difficulties you experience in the practice of psychotherapy?

a.l.   One interesting problem that stands out is the type of clients who, objectively speaking, have no reason to disparage themselves, but tend to denigrate themselves excessively. It's easy if somebody comes into therapy and is very negative for clear-cut or obvious reasons; you can see that they are in fact making tremendous blunders, or enter into very unfortunate relationships and you can see why they feel badly about themselves. You can tell these people that there is no need to judge themselves entirely negatively for having made these blunders. You can agree to work on ways and means of getting out of their destructive patterns and thereby foster better feelings and more positive self-concepts. But when a person doesn't have, as I said, any objective reason to feel down on themselves and yet are prone to enormous self-downing, I find it very hard to get through to such individuals in most cases.

w.d.   What is the difficulty there?

a.l.   The difficulty there is that often when you take a full history either they have such incredible standards for themselves, or have absorbed so many pejorative put-downs that they have a distorted view of what they can expect of themselves or others, and there is no way of budging these perceptions.

w.d.   So it is as if their attitude towards themselves has become very entrenched and it is difficult for you to produce any shift in that rigid attitude.

a.l.   I find this to be the case with some excessively religious individuals who are very unhappy and come for help because of their unhappiness, and yet embrace a theological position that espouses unhappiness as an entry point into heaven. This leads to a catch-22. The more miserable you are in this life, the happier you will be in the hereafter. So if you believe in that, why not be happy because you are so sad? But the ones who come for therapy say, in effect, 'How can I feel less miserable and not lose my place in heaven when I die?' Many of these people are unwilling or unable to let go of these entrenched ideas.

w.d.   Do you think that there are particular problems or difficulties that multimodal therapists might experience with clients more frequently than therapists from other schools?

a.l.   I have been struck by some therapists who are existential or experiential in outlook and who do not experience these problems because they view the entire process and outcome of psychotherapy in a totally different light. So they don't measure change in terms of symptom reduction, increased pleasure in life, improved social skills, and better occupational conditions. Rather they talk in terms of an I–thou encounter with their clients and as long as they sit in their offices week after week and reach out and talk about the meaning of life, and examine values, feelings and experiences with their clients, this is fine for these clinicians. And they therefore certainly don't run into the frustrations to which I am referring.

w.d.   So they wouldn't even label these issues as difficulties, it would just become a part of the ongoing experiential process.

a.l.   Correct, because the goal as far as these existential/ experiential therapists are concerned is for people to grow in their awareness, and that's such a vague term that it is difficult to know when it's not happening, and many people are seduced by this type of process. I don't want to say that there are no people who derive benefit from this because certainly there is a market for it. But this is almost a polar opposite of what goes on in a multimodal formulation.

I was recently on a panel with an experiential therapist, Alvin Mahrer, and when he was asked how he would deal with complaints, such as phobias, compulsions, sexual inadequacies, his answer was 'I never ever focus on such complaints. My patients and I sit with our eyes closed and we discuss our innermost feelings, thoughts and sensations, we get in touch with our sense of awareness, we become focused and centred.' These were the kinds of answers he gave. Consequently he would not experience the frustration of a multimodal therapist whose goal would be entirely different, aimed at reducing suffering, eliminating intrusive compulsions and phobias, enhancing sexual pleasuring and so on.

w.d.   Do you have clients who come to you seeking an existential encounter rather than programmatic treatment?

a.l.   Sometimes, yes.

w.d.   And how do you respond?

a.l.   My response to such individuals is that it is easy enough to provide them with the I–thou encounter they seem to desire. I had a woman in therapy who is a brilliant philosopher and it soon became quite apparent to me that what she wanted from me was the opportunity to explore her feelings rather than to modify any of her behaviours. She was a contemplative individual, not action-oriented in terms of what we had said previously. And this was very much experiential treatment where we would discuss her ongoing experiences *vis-à-vis* her husband, her son, her work, her deeper feelings of life and the meaning of life and mortality. These were the issues she wanted to talk about. So I listened, I reflected, I asked questions, and thought, 'Gee, I can see why some of these existential therapists like to do this all the time, because it is a lot easier than what I do with most other people.' By the way, she was a satisfied customer when 'therapy' ended.

w.d.   So you are happy to take on clients who wish to pursue more existentially oriented goals?

a.l.   I don't mind, right.

w.d.   In fact you quite enjoy it.

a.l.   Correct.

w.d.   Are there any other situations where other therapists from other persuasions might not experience the problems and difficulties that multimodal therapists might face?

a.l.   There are so many approaches. There are literally hundreds of systems of psychotherapy and some of them are highly focused. For example in an approach like rebirthing, there is a very definite sequential order of events that people go through, but I couldn't see those therapists even facing the problems that I am discussing because they have such different objectives in mind.

I am also thinking of certain people who call themselves Gestalt therapists who are very eager for people to become more authentic and to communicate at a spontaneous gut level, and achieve that to their satisfaction and often to the patients' satisfaction. Again, the focus there is not necessarily the same range of overt and covert change patterns that multimodal therapists aim for. It's a lot harder, you see to work the way I think one needs to work. This is why I think that if you ask therapists why they chose to practise Jungian, Freudian, Adlerian, Ericksonian, or another kind of therapy, rather than embrace a multimodal orientation, they don't say because there are data to show that their way of proceeding has proven most effective. They say, 'I like it; it makes sense to me; that was taught to me; these have been my role models; I had that kind of therapy and it helped me.' Those are the kinds of answers they give. From a scientific standpoint one might look askance at these reasons.

w.d.   That brings us on to a different kind of problem or difficulty and that refers to obstacles to the wider acceptance of multimodal therapy. You have begun to touch on this theme, and I wonder if you could now address it more fully.

a.l.   It is my subjective impression that therapists prefer to do things that they are comfortable with. We are all limited and delimited creatures, and there are those who would argue that they prefer to specialize in one or two things that they do exceptionally well, rather than do ten things reasonably well. I think that patients become short-changed by that, because as Abraham Maslow pointed out many years ago, if the only tool you have is a hammer, you treat everything like a nail. Now I would advance that metaphor and say that if you have a hammer and a saw and a screwdriver, you can do a lot more than just having a hammer alone. But if you also have a Phillips screwdriver, sometimes this is even better than just an ordinary screwdriver, and if on top of that you have a saw and a plane and a drill, you can do even more things. But what this implies is that you know how to use these other tools. How much easier to say, 'My speciality is using the hammer: I can hammer things in better than anyone, it's wonderful', as opposed to 'I will have to learn how to use power saws and power drills' – which is much more demanding. So multimodal therapy says, equip yourself with as many tools as possible and this places quite a demand on the clinician. We can't be expert in the use of them all, but it is my contention that ten tools used well will give you a far better and wider outcome than three tools used or brandished magnificently. So clinicians, I think, will resist that and rather favour the one, two or three specialized procedures, that they can do very well because it makes life easier for them and they can rationalize away their failures.

w.d.   Right, so what you are saying is that the effective practice of multimodal therapy really is quite demanding. One has to equip oneself with various tools and constantly be on the lookout for new tools. Whereas, in contrast, you consider that the attitude which is more prevalent in our field can be summed up thus: 'No, that's too complicated, let me use what is comfortable or what I am used to'.

a.l.   If you look at the field you will see how many therapists these days like family therapy. Now of course there are many, many ways of performing family therapy, which in itself is a problem, because rival factions develop and numerous unsubstantiated claims are made for and against one or another particular kind of family therapy. The client who sees a family therapist who is, say, a structuralist will receive that approach to family therapy, whether or not he or she needs it, because that is what the practitioner does well.

People also like mystery and they have deified the late Milton Erickson. His vast number of followers are mesmerized by the anecdotes, metaphors, stories for the third ear and other kinds of pseudo-magical procedures that are being churned out. Whereas multimodal therapy is hard work.

I was reading through a book that was edited by Wedding and Corsini (1989) in which I have a chapter; the book is called *Case Studies in Psychotherapy*. The chapter that I wrote in this book which is an examplar of the multimodal approach is called 'The case of George'. When I read through the case of George, I felt exhausted, because it was such hard work getting this fellow to change and become a fully functioning human being. I repeat, it was hard work. There was nothing in it that was inspired or inspiring or magical; it was hard, systematic, comprehensive, broad-based work. And when I finished reading the case, I felt tired because I remembered how exhausting it was. By contrast some of the other case studies in that book by therapists of different persuasions depict therapy which seemed to be fun, a game, and dealt with all kinds of amusing abstractions. I am not sure how much true and genuine help accrued, but certainly the therapist had a wonderful time.

I have had prominent therapists say to me, in all candour, that they would not work multimodally because it wouldn't be as much fun as what they do. To which I have responded by saying that I didn't know that we therapists are in the business for our own enjoyment, as opposed to helping our clients. But multimodal therapy is like orthopaedic surgery. I often use the analogy, a little far fetched, of a man with a broken arm where the orthopaedic surgeon can't get into the operating room to set his bone because the operating room is busy, and so while they are waiting, week after week, they talk about love, sex, poetry and the meaning of life. After the man is finally wheeled into the operating room, they do an X-ray and the bone has healed. To give credit for the healing to the discussions about love, sex, poetry and the meaning of life is a little ill advised, but this is what happens in some psychotherapies. People remit spontaneously, people get over their problems for many, many reasons, and in the mean time their therapists have been getting them to jump up and down, and contemplate their navels, and when they get better, the therapists falsely assume it is because of what they did. Whereas the gains might be for reasons other than the procedures employed.

w.d.   So what you are saying is that the effective practice of multimodal therapy is demanding, it's not necessarily intrinsically exciting and full of fun; in fact it's damned hard work. And in a sense you wonder how many therapists are willing to submit themselves to that kind of demanding regime.

a.l.   Yes, and I can see why many therapists get seduced by other approaches that are easier, more fun.

w.d.   To what extent do you think that multimodal therapy may also place demands on clients?

a.l.   It should be much less demanding on the client, than on the therapist, because the skilful therapist paces it accordingly. People who don't understand the multimodal approach incorrectly think that we impose on the person such a tremendous burden that they will retreat from the therapy, and throw their hands up in horror feeling that they can't possibly do all that is required of them. But although we usually try to cover the entire BASIC I.D., the clients don't feel overwhelmed, so I don't think that they experience the process as enervating. But I know that the therapists do. I say this because there are quite a number of therapists in this area who practise, as I do, and when we get together, the discussion often touches on the fatigue that we therapists feel, and the need we have to take vacations and get away from the burden of the work. I am aware that many therapists contend that performing therapy should be fun. Now there are some clients with whom it is distinctly pleasurable to work and who are most enjoyable. But for the most part I claim that effective therapy is tough going, and that the fun or gratification comes from really proving to be helpful in the end.

w.d.   How do *you* manage to cope with fatigue and the potential problem of burn-out?

a.l.   By not being greedy and not seeing too many people a week and by recognizing my limitations and calling for help from colleagues, when I think it will be useful.

w.d.   So you pace yourself and you also draw upon the resources of others.

a.l.   That's well put.

w.d.   Just to round off this discussion on problems and difficulties: you have mentioned situations whereby therapists from other

persuasions may not encounter difficulties that multimodal therapists may face. Are there also circumstances where you consider
that multimodal therapists might not encounter problems and
difficulties faced by these other therapists?

A.L.   Yes, I'll tell you one of the main problems that I hear other
therapists experience, that does not seem to be true of the way my
colleagues and I work. Many of these other therapists seem to have
tremendous termination problems. Indeed there are many books
and chapters written on how to go about the process of terminating
with clients. I think this is because many of these other clinicians
practise a brand of therapy that makes the patient very dependent
upon them. The paradox here is that a multimodal therapist is apt
to be far more interactive and real with his or her clients than some
other therapists and yet we don't foster the kind of dependency that
we see happening in other therapeutic approaches. So that's one
difficulty some of them have.

The other difficulty that ties into this is the manner in which
some people act out in the therapy where they get into transference
neuroses and the therapists experience a good deal of problems
aimed at them. This I think is because they have failed to address
the clients' specific problems, they haven't been goal directed or
task specific and they have become so embroiled in process
variables and interactions with the patient, that suddenly they
become the subject of the patient's attacks. We in multimodal
therapy seldom see this because we remain essentially problem-
focused, searching for solutions in concert with the patient. We
also downplay the central significance that some therapists attach
to the doctor–patient relationship. We portray ourselves as purely
catalytic. We say 'What is important is the way you relate to your
friends, your lovers, your employers, your employees, etc. I am
here to help you, but as a person, I am not one of your significant
others'. We don't get embroiled in some of these tremendous
transference battles that we see happening in other schools of
thought.

VIEWS ON CURRENT
APPROACHES TO
PSYCHOTHERAPY

WINDY DRYDEN   Now I want to discuss your views on the contemporary psychotherapy scene. There are literally hundreds of different
approaches to psychotherapy, but for the purposes of this interview I would like to focus on the mainstream approaches, as well as
some of the less traditional approaches which are currently in
vogue. Let's begin by discussing your views on psychodynamic
approaches to psychotherapy. What do you see as some of their
strengths and weaknesses?

ARNOLD LAZARUS   I suppose under the rubric of psychodynamic, the
three that stand out are Freudian psychoanalysis, Adlerian individual psychotherapy and Jungian analytical psychotherapy, although
there are dozens of psychoanalytic derivatives or offshoots. In my
opinion *Current Psychotherapies* (fourth edition) edited by Raymond Corsini and Danny Wedding (1989), wherein they present
fourteen *mainstream* approaches, is the best source that permits
the reader to understand and compare different orientations that
are in current use. Let's start off with psychoanalysis and ask what
data exist that show that psychoanalysis for any specific problem is
ever the treatment of choice? I don't know of any. Yet there are
people who are enchanted by the process: by the very idea of lying
on a couch and free associating. In some circles, classic psychoanalysis still has a wide appeal, and people of great prominence in
motion pictures, in sporting and other public arenas are well-
known analysands who tout the quintessential virtues of that
process. Nevertheless, when it comes to anything scientific, I can't
do better than quote a recent editorial by Paul Mullen (1989) in the
Australian and New Zealand Journal of Psychiatry. His editorial
was entitled 'Psychoanalysis: a creed in decline' and the abstract
says:

Psychoanalysis is in decline. Its methods disbar it from serious consideration as a natural science and its claims of therapeutic efficacy are in tatters. The role it performed earlier in the century as part of the narrative knowledge of western culture is in eclipse. Trainees in psychiatry are still, however, on occasion, seduced by its faded charms to their detriment. The time has come to relegate psychoanalysis to its proper place as a moment in the historical development of psychiatry and a ripple in 20th-century western culture.

(Mullen 1989: 17)

Mullen then goes on for several pages to underscore the fact that psychoanalysis as a treatment modality has certainly failed miserably. Its continual prominence may be viewed as a form of religion rather than as a science of psychotherapy.

w.d.   What are your views on the briefer versions of psychodynamic psychotherapy?

a.l.   It is clear that brief therapy is an area of specialization that would probably not exist were it not for the dominance of the psychoanalytic orientation during the major part of this century. Despite the profusion of therapeutic orientations, in many quarters psychotherapy is still synonymous with psychoanalytic or psychodynamic therapy. Brief therapy as a speciality seems to have arisen in the psychodynamic context although history is replete with rapid remissions from all kinds of ministrations.

Perhaps the situation would have been less murky if psychodynamic or psychoanalytic therapy had been referred to all these years as protracted therapy and its more recent development designated less protracted or briefer therapy. What actually happened was that psychodynamic therapists first decried the newer short-term therapies as superficial and inferior, even dangerous. Or else they dismissed them and said they were just designed for those people who are not healthy, not integrated enough for real psychoanalysis. They then modified their product, and with good reason. Brief dynamic therapy satisfies the growing time and economic constraints imposed by consumers and third-party payers; it meets the challenge of literally hundreds of competing approaches, helps boost the decimated enrolment in analytic training institutes and makes outcome research more meaningful. But my personal reaction to brief psychodynamic therapy is that it is an attempt to make an archaic model work more efficiently, rather like hitting a nail harder and more rapidly instead of putting it in the right place and using power tools.

So what has happened is that demands of society have led these people to develop these short-term, time-limited or brief forms of psychodynamic therapies. But data are now being gathered. One of the researchers, Dr H. Davanloo, has videotaped his sessions. These tapes reveal that he is very active, unlike the classical psychoanalyst, and inadvertently, in my opinion, uses some rational-emotive techniques, behavioural techniques and cognitive techniques, although he wouldn't label them as such. They seem to get better results than has been true of classical psychoanalysis, but still it's rather haphazard as I see it; it is not truly systematic, and not as comprehensive as brief multimodal approaches, but at least it doesn't take years and years while people get milked of all their money. So that's my overall response to some of the briefer dynamic therapies.

w.d.   Let's move on to your views on Jungian therapy.

a.l.   Well, Windy, let me say immediately that I don't see Jungian therapy as therapy at all. I see it as some art form, some mystical encounter, some religious experience, because the Jungian therapist is consumed with dreams and symbols and phylogenetic unconscious memories and racial cross-cultural symbols, and the animus and anima that are said to operate like autonomous personalities. I see very little that this has to do with therapy, but regard the Jungian approach as a religious art form. I couldn't imagine myself referring a patient to a Jungian for therapy unless this person was functioning very well, and desired to have some sort of an enlightening mystical, consciousness-expanding experience such as the Jungians claim to provide. But I don't think of this as therapy in the sense of helping people in distress, effecting change, overcoming problems or anything like that.

w.d.   What about Adlerian therapy?

a.l.   The Adlerian approach is one that is closest to my own thinking. I think that Adler as a theorist has been greatly undersold, that somehow Freud and Jung squeezed him out, whereas he is the one that should have been the hero, in the past fifty years, because he innovated many psycho-educational programmes and processes. I have noticed something about the Adlerians I have met. They all seem to be very kind people. They treat their patients with inordinate respect and are often very effective by virtue of the fact that they are educational and action-oriented. There is great wisdom in Adler's writings, but the overall orientation lacks the systemization that is called for. But many of my ideas about life, people, education, society and so forth have been heavily influenced by my readings of Adler's work and by some time I spent at the Marlborough Day Hospital in London when I was a student. Dr Joshua Bierer headed up the hospital and he was an Adlerian. I am far more positive about the Adlerian approach than I am about the Freudian and Jungian approach.

w.d.   Let's move on to the humanistic and existential approaches to psychotherapy. Perhaps we could start by looking at your views on person-centred therapy.

a.l.   The person-centred therapy that Carl Rogers developed seems to be a most useful backdrop for most clinicians. That is to say I think that he was correct in researching some of the most important facilitative conditions by underscoring the need for empathy, genuineness and unconditional positive regard. This provides a good starting-point, a constructive context, or a creative therapeutic climate. But it is decidedly insufficient for overcoming most problems, especially serious ones. As I said earlier it is merely the soil into which we need specific techniques to be inserted that will take root. Again there are certainly no data that the person-centred approach alleviates tics, phobias, compulsions, habit disorders, obsessions, panic disorders, or any host of other complaints, but what it does, and certainly does well, is to facilitate the passage of young college students into the next phase of their identity. It started out in a college setting and has very little relevance I think to the world at large and to most of the problems that face us. So I see person-centred therapy merely as a useful backdrop and, from time to time, I am very Rogerian. Where I see in my chameleon sense that the patient requires some warmth, some fatherly attention, and little else, then he or she gets it. In most instances we then have to move on to other things that are far more productive.

w.d.   How does this tie into the existential approach of people like Rollo May, or Irving Yalom?

a.l.   The interesting thing about existential psychotherapy is that its adherents admit that it is not a specific technical approach; it doesn't present any new rules for the conduct of therapy. What existential therapy does is ask questions, questions that all of us can resonate to, questions about the nature of the human being, the nature of anxiety, despair, grief, loneliness, isolation and anomie. It deals with issues of creativity and love. They seem to assume that by exploring these kinds of issues that emphasize the understanding of personal meaning, of deep human feelings, patients will somehow come to terms with their lot in life. Again, I see that as useful for some people, and as part of a multimodal approach, I will discuss the heavy issues with individuals who so desire, and often they do come away with some feeling of peace or enrichment or cosmic fulfilment. But as a treatment on its own, I would ask whether there are any data to show that it can do better than other approaches. Clearly the answer is 'No'.

w.d. What is your opinion of some of the approaches to therapy that have emerged from the so-called fourth force of psychology, namely transpersonal psychology.

a.l. Frankly I have never fully understood what the transpersonal therapists are all about. From what I have read, they seem to espouse spiritual, mystical, esoteric notions. They love the word 'transcendental', and they talk about out-of-body awareness. It strikes me as a Jungian derivative in some ways but attracts those people I think who are searching for something even more unscientific, because the transpersonal approach, as I understand it, does not deal specifically or systematically with problems, procedures and programmes to work through or mitigate well-defined problems. It is a global, spiritual way of processing information.

As Albert Ellis and Raymond Yeager (1989) pointed out in their book *Why Some Therapies Don't Work* there are numerous dangers of transpersonal psychology. One of the problems with transpersonal approaches is that they oppose the tenets of humanism, in that they emphasize that our lives on this earth should be lived so that we can achieve happiness in an after-life, or a heavenly existence, and they talk in terms of ultimate reward, sacrifices, martyrdom, and a lot of sabotaging of ongoing pleasures for the greater benefit of an after-life that is eternal. So this is an approach that tends to foster, according to Ellis and Yeager, an anti-human censorship, a type of fascism that can easily escalate into terrorism, religious war and genocide. We need to avoid those who fanatically prescribe in the name of some supreme power, what his or her zealous followers should do. But the entire transpersonal approach does not deny reality and many responsible transpersonal therapists do not preach about the wonders of a great after-life. But most of their ideas are antithetical to what I consider science, effective therapy and humanistic living. It is again a polar opposite of what I stand for.

w.d.   Now let's discuss your views on the current trends within
behaviour therapy and cognitive-behaviour therapy. This is, of
course, the tradition with which you have been most closely
associated in the past. Are you still happy to be associated with this
tradition?   *MULTIMODAL*

a.l.   Yes, although I see myself as broader, more technically eclectic
and more flexible than most of my behavioural and cognitive-
behavioural confreres. I do identify most strongly with the
cognitive-behavioural approach, because it is grounded in research, because it deals with cause–effect sequences and because it
represents an honest attempt to try and answer the question of who
or what is best, for each individual client. One of the big mistakes
that some sophisticated researchers have made is to conclude from
meta-analyses (e.g. the work of Smith, Glass and Miller 1980) that
there are no specific problems that call for prescribed treatments,
that no one method is superior to another. If you reinterpret a lot of
the meta-analyses more carefully you will see that behavioural
approaches are the ones that are superior to all others across the
board (e.g. Shapiro and Shapiro 1983). This is not surprising,
because the behavioural approaches are the ones that encourage
people to think differently and perform differently, which I think
are the two major ingredients of change.

Contemporary behaviour therapy is marked by a diversity of
views and continues to spawn a broad range of procedures. It had
started out in a somewhat narrow fashion but contemporary
behaviour therapy is very much broader today than it was ten years
ago, but it remains predicated on the seminal assumption that
clinical practice should adhere firmly to the principles and findings
of experimental psychology. Now the nice thing about the
cognitive-behavioural approach is that its philosophy does not
preclude the use of concepts and treatment methods borrowed
from areas not directly connected with experimental psychology,
like systems theory, communications training or, of course,
psychopharmacology. Initially behaviour therapy was defined as
the clinical application of modern learning theory, but today this is
too narrow, although there are still some people in the field who
don't seem to realize this.

w.d.   Are you concerned at all with the way the field of behaviour
therapy and cognitive-behavioural therapy is developing?

a.l.   What really concerns me most about behaviour therapy is that
people seem to be fragmenting and specializing. For instance the
discipline called 'behavioural medicine', which is enormously

popular in this country, is a case in point. What appears to be happening there is that people are now becoming specialists, which I think is unwise. We need so much more information before it makes sense to specialize. Nevertheless, you get people who are biofeedback specialists or who specialize in the treatment of cardiovascular disorders, or who apply the principles of learning to other very specific populations, and there is a certain narrowness that has crept back into the individual practitioner's activities. This is in line with what I was saying earlier about the multimodal orientation not being as popular as those that give the clinician a sense of expertise along a narrow path. I find this narrowness, this pseudo-expertise, creeping into many areas. Take a look at the journal articles that are being published currently in the behavioural and cognitive-behavioural journals. They are so highly focused and specialized that they have almost no relevance for the general practitioner. Editors would far rather publish an article that describes an *ABA* design with an alcoholic who was trying out different kinds of brandies in different concentrations, than it would a piece that deals with a broad multimodal approach to a wide array of difficulties because you cannot obtain such immaculate controls. So one of my main concerns is that the scientific tenets that set behavioural approaches apart from the other orientations and make them so attractive also produce the negative fragmentation and atomistic quality that I am complaining about. I read so many papers that seem so molecular, so minor in importance, that I come away feeling frustrated. I would like to see more, let's call them chunkier bits of information, coming out of the cognitive-behaviour therapy literature.

w.d.   I'd like to discuss specifically your views on two specific approaches within the cognitive-behavioural tradition, namely rational-emotive therapy and Beck's cognitive therapy. If you were faced with the choice of practising either rational-emotive therapy (RET) or cognitive therapy which one would you choose to practise?

a.l.   It's too difficult for me to answer this question because whenever I have endeavoured, either in writing or in discussion with Beck, Ellis, and other rational-emotive and cognitive therapists, to delineate what seems to me to be the parameters and the boundaries of their respective approaches, I am always told this is incorrect, and that they are in fact far more pervasive and broad-based than I give them credit for being.

w.d.   How do you respond to that?

A.L.   I respond to that by saying that theoretically there is nothing to stop RET practitioners or any of Beck's followers from using any of the multimodal methods, but in fact their scope is far less exhaustive. Ellis's pat answer to this is 'But we do that anyhow, and have done that years before you even thought of it'.

In my piece on 'The practice of rational-emotive therapy' in the book edited by Michael Bernard and Raymond DiGiuseppe (1989) called *Inside Rational-Emotive Therapy* I argued that if you look at what is actually done by many cognitive and rational-emotive therapists, you will see that they do not employ or draw upon the imagery, sensory, interpersonal, affective and biological domains as extensively as they claim. They have a penchant to stay in the cognitive area almost exclusively at times and certainly, in my view, to overdo it quite often. This is a view that both Ellis and Beck have argued against, but they have not persuaded me that I am wrong in holding to this notion.

W.D.   So once again you would fault them because of their lack of breadth in that they neglect modalities which you consider to be important to assess and treat.

A.L.   Yes, not only are certain modalities in my view at times glossed over or neglected, but even those that are addressed are attended to in a somewhat narrow way. For example take imagery. While Ellis and many rational-emotive therapists make use of imagery (they have devised what is called 'rational-emotive imagery' and they use some other kinds of imagery methods), I doubt if they use more than four or five different imagery techniques. I am not sure if cognitive therapists of Beck's persuasion employ much formal mental imagery training. However, in mulitmodal therapy there are at least ten or twelve different imagery techniques that we draw upon. Let me repeat that there is nothing to stop rational-emotive therapists or cognitive therapists from doing the same, but they are too inclined to dwell on 'left brain' ideas to the neglect of 'right brain' images. I find them too narrow in practice.

W.D.   What is your view of family therapy?

A.L.   Family therapy means different things to different people; there are many forms of family therapy. The family therapy that was practised by Nathan Ackerman is different from that of Murray Bowen, or Salvador Minuchin, or Carl Whittaker, or Jay Haley, to mention some of the leading figures in family therapy. They all differ from one another and are all very much at odds with someone like Gerald Patterson, who is a behavioural family therapist. So once more I don't think that there is a systematic body of knowledge that could be called family therapy. What has emerged is that it is often very useful to see people in a family context, and a multimodal clinician will certainly make that determination. However, instead of saying as many family therapists do, 'I work with families', the multimodal therapist will swing the focus of attention back and forth between the individual and his or her parts and the individual in his or her social setting. So there are times when we consider that family therapy is indicated. For example we might be seeing an individual who keeps talking about problems with family members and the issue that is then raised in the therapy is that it might facilitate matters if they were present, so we could get their direct input and deal with some of these interpersonal issues. To my mind there is nothing terribly mysterious or wonderful about that.

w.d.   Multimodal therapy really emerged from the behavioural and cognitive tradition. Consequently would you say that the way multimodal therapists practise therapy within a family context, draws most upon social learning approaches to family therapy?

a.l.   Yes. Let's take a particular case. The point I want to show is how simple and straightforward 'family sessions' can be. I was working with a young woman of 28 who was very upset about the fact that she saw her father as somebody who felt utterly disappointed in her. She also had a number of resentments towards her mother that she had difficulty expressing. She and I discussed these issues, did some role-playing, and I encouraged her to approach her parents and express her feelings. But she did not do so and experienced some difficulty and reluctance. After further discussion, I suggested we bring them into therapy; she agreed, the parents came on in, and we discussed these matters quite openly. The father unequivocally stated that he was not the least bit disappointed in his daughter; on the contrary, he emphasized how proud he was of her. The daughter became very emotional about this and she and her father developed a different understanding and style of interaction there and then. Next I encouraged the daughter to tell her mother about her additional concerns. The daughter found it easier to do that with me as the referee. She and the mother had a very meaningful conversation before the session ended. The daughter came back (individually) to the next session and reported that the family session had been a pivotal turning-point.

Indeed after the family session, she continued to make significant progress. So there is a simple case in point, where I involved the family system in an obvious, straightforward, common-sense way.

w.d.   You have noted the diverse nature of approaches within the family therapy field. What is your view of the current status of family therapy?

a.l.   My view is that most of it is anecdotal, and there are very few, if any, findings that are research-based or data-based. We have a tremendous number of family therapy enthusiasts, we have some very charismatic personable bright people in that field, many of whom I am sure are excellent clinicians by virtue of their own artistic skills, but the field as a whole strikes me as one that is rather fragmented and chaotic.

w.d.   There has been a recent interest in approaches to psychotherapy which have their foundation in the work of Milton Erickson and in neurolinguistic programming. What is your view of these developments?

a.l.   Here again, my feeling is that there are very bright capable people who are making very cogent points about several effective interventions. Erickson himself was a very gifted and inventive clinician. Some of his followers have taken his ideas a lot further, but again we are not provided with a body of cohesive or coherent knowledge, but we are given a pot-pourri of notions, concepts and ideologies to draw upon. There is nothing wrong with a smorgasbord. My objection, however, is that a lot of the people who say they are Ericksonians, do not have a systematic scientific grounding, do not have an adherence to, and an understanding of social learning theory, do not appreciate the importance of concepts like modelling, vicarious learning, self-efficacy and so forth, and are extremely enamoured of the inventive strategies that emerge from their discipline and apply them willy-nilly, often to the detriment of people who require something entirely different. As a multimodal therapist with technical eclecticism as the backdrop, I do not buy into any of their theories, but can borrow any of their techniques. But I find myself distressed when they present what they do as complete therapies when what they have offered, I submit, are some very useful strategies and ideas. The same could be said of Gestalt therapy, psychodrama, transactional analysis and bioenergetic analysis, to mention a few other approaches. Many of these approaches have an enormous following, because of the limited and highly focused appeal that we keep referring to.

w.d.   To sum up what you seem to be saying is that the approaches we have discussed all make a contribution in certain restricted areas, but they lack comprehensiveness and breadth. You even see cognitive-behavioural approaches to psychotherapy as incomplete and what you seem to be saying is that only multimodal therapy is comprehensive. Am I correct?

A.L. What multimodal therapy is trying to achieve is a systematic and comprehensive approach. It is not a school or a closed system. It is an eclectic endeavour to avoid getting seduced by any single orientation.

W.D. But you don't consider that the other approaches that we have discussed are working towards that degree of comprehensiveness?

A.L. I do not. I see the other approaches as having definite cut-off points. They stop dead at certain points. They do not look beyond certain boundaries. I have positioned myself outside of all of that and keep wondering how can we draw on all of these useful approaches without buying into a mishmash of theories, and ending up in a state of confusion. Theoretical integrationism, as I see it, is an unfortunate way to go at present. To believe that we can extract the best theories and conceptual underpinnings from the myriad approaches before us strikes me as beyond our ken. This is too much, too confusing, and it cannot be accomplished for many reasons, not the least of which is that many of the theories are incompatible, they rest on paradigms that are totally different, and their frameworks are epistemologically dissimilar. But we can be technically eclectic or as you have expressed it, theoretically consistent (Dryden 1987) and yet draw upon techniques of proven efficacy from any discipline. My sense is that if we don't do that, we are going to be very limited in our effectiveness. But I would submit that the scientist cannot afford to be eclectic; the scientist needs to check on one or two variables at a time, to distil the active ingredients and then the clinician can take that and use it. So the multimodal approach is one that does not synthesize theories, but systematizes techniques across disciplines.

W.D. In your view, what is the current status of multimodal therapy within the general area of eclecticism and integration?

A.L. I think it fits in very well with the systematic prescriptive therapies that have become, as you pointed out, a high interest group in recent years. In other words, it recognizes 'treatments of choice' for specific problems. The very fact that there is a Society for the Exploration of Psychotherapy Integration (SEPI) points to the fact that therapists of diverse persuasions are now willing to sit down and talk with one another, to trade ideas and to try and achieve a synergistic strengthening by virtue of pooling and combining their strategies.

W.D.   In answering that question you see multimodal therapy most closely associated with those who are interested in developing a prescriptive approach to psychotherapy. But what interest do those within SEPI have in multimodal therapy?

A.L.   You have touched on something that I think is endemic and that is the fact that many of the people are very busy pedalling their own wares and remain, if not uninterested, certainly disinterested in what other people are offering. So we are getting various brands of eclectisism, and I would say that if there is one organization that knows most about multimodal thinking, it would be the SEPI organization. But I would also say that there are I suppose at least a third of its members who wouldn't know the difference between multimodal ideas and any other brand of eclecticism.

W.D.   If I am not mistaken, what you seem to be alluding to is that there seems to be a similar development within the movement towards eclecticism and integration that has occurred within the larger field of psychotherapy. Specifically that we are now seeing a proliferation of different approaches to eclecticism and integration.

A.L.   That is correct. In fact I think I would be quoting you correctly when I say that you in a critique (Dryden 1986) have pointed out that there was in fact a danger of developing as many eclectic orientations as there are competing systems of psychotherapy on the current market. You have stated how unfortunate that would be. Instead we need to try to foster an approach that would develop a systematic, consistent, responsible prescriptive eclecticism that most people would adhere to.

W.D.   How optimistic are you that this may occur in the future?

A.L.   I am uncertain. As I have already pointed out, there is a penchant for people to promote their own wares to the exclusion of others. They may win out, so that instead of people truly absorbing effective methods and ideas from another, they will continue to push their own brands of eclecticism. I hope I am wrong about that.

W.D.   So your prediction is that the hope for movement towards integration where we in a sense either come to talk a common language or agree on common change principles and intervention principles is not likely to be realized.

A.L.   I can't say that I am very optimistic of that happening, but I can at least report one positive trend. When I first wrote about technical eclecticism in 1967, I received widespread opposition from behavioural and psychodynamic clinicians alike. But today, many former detractors are seeing that eclecticism is not necessarily the enemy of science, and that a systematic technically eclectic position can add to knowledge.

| 5

DOS AND DON'TS AND SACRED COWS

WINDY DRYDEN   One of your recent interests has been to develop a list of 'dos and don'ts' that have been passed down from generation to generation in the field of psychotherapy but have, by and large, remained unchallenged. Before we consider these in detail, could you say a little about how you became interested in this subject?

ARNOLD LAZARUS   I found that most of my training consisted of being told what I was *not* to do. I was handed a long list of 'don'ts' and 'nevers' by my trainers and supervisors. Unfortunately this is still true today in many centres, where students are trained *never* to do this, *always* to do that, *not to* say this, *not to* say that, and so forth. This runs counter to individual differences, to idiosyncratic needs, and undermines the uniqueness that people are all about. Now let me say at the outset, that there are a couple of absolute don'ts to which I subscribe. One of them is 'Don't engage in sexual contact with your clients'. This is not because I am a prude; but frankly I do not think that sex and therapy or counselling can mix. There are some clinicians who challenge that view, and have claimed that in fact positive gains have accrued when they have broken this taboo, but I am not willing to even entertain that because I think that the risks far outweigh the advantages. The risks here are those of exploitation, all kinds of false expectations, ambiguities, confusion of roles, and the violation of trust. So that certainly is one of my nevers and absolute don'ts. The other one is not to attack one's clients as human beings, that is not to put them down as people *in toto*, and avoid ridicule, scorn and derision. Would you like me to talk first about what I think some of the main mistakes are that therapists make that produce problems before we challenge some of the sacred cows?

W.D.   Let's do that.

A.L.   I think that there are some therapists who are noxious or destructive. Sometimes bad therapy is carried out by well-intentioned but poorly trained practitioners who apply incorrect techniques, or perhaps they apply the correct techniques, but do so poorly. But one of the destructive things that I think clinicians sometimes use are labels. They tell their clients that they have a passive personality, or a narcissistic personality disorder, and they use other labels that are very destructive. When therapists display disgust, disdain, impatience, blaming, disrespect, intolerance or induce guilt in their patients, this is when I think the most negative effects ensue. For example, if a therapist says 'Why didn't you wake up and do something before your son got hooked on drugs?', we have an example of a guilt-inducing statement, that is not meritorious in any sense. Or saying to a patient 'Well, you made a mess of that situation and now you expect me to pick up the pieces!' is only blaming the client and is of little (if any) help. These things happen more often than we want to believe. There are some therapists who are blatantly insensitive, and really ought to be in another field of endeavour.

When therapists are inaccurate, or when they fail to appreciate a client's feelings, or are highly inappropriate in timing their remarks, unfortunate consequences usually ensue. One of my clients reported that his previous therapist said, 'You have come a long way during the past eighteen months but if you terminate therapy now, you will be right back to square one before you know it.' Attempts to foster dependency are all too frequent. Not too long ago, there was an edition of the *New York Magazine*, where the cover had a person chained to an analyst's couch: the title was 'Prisoners of Psychotherapy' and the therapists interviewed anonymously said, 'Well, I hang on to patients as long as I can, because if somebody leaves me there is a gap in my appointment book and there goes my fee for the tennis club for that month, or my car payments suffer'. It is most unfortunate for people to be kept in therapy longer than they need to be. At a less damaging level we have instances of irrelevant questions, confusing remarks and false reassurance. It's just as bad to give false reassurance as it is to blame or condemn; you want to be honest with your clients. So those are some of the mistakes I think that therapists make and the public would be far better served if they did not make those kinds of mistakes.

But now let's get back to the first part of your question, and let me share with you some of the don'ts that I was given that I have now violated. They aren't in any particular order of importance. Let's start with one, which was '*Don't give advice*'. Now a lot of people assume that if you give advice you are somehow truncating the client's own sense of self, that he or she will then be dependent upon you and the cliché is 'You have not taught them how to fish, you have merely given them a fish to eat'. If you withhold advice then somehow they will generate solutions for themselves. On the contrary, without receiving advice they may never see the light. What I have found in my practice is that when I give advice, clients come to believe that they arrived at the conclusions without input from me. I may say, 'I would advise you to discuss the situation with your brother because you will feel very guilty in the long run if you don't do that. This is my advice.' And the person may answer, 'No, I don't think I want to discuss it with my brother, I don't think it will work', so we let it go. Two or three weeks later, the person comes into therapy and says, 'You know what I've decided? I have decided I want to have a discussion with my brother. If I don't I will probably end up feeling guilty and so I have made up my mind to go ahead and we are going to meet on Friday night and discuss the matter.' They have now owned it; I have planted the seed and it grew over time although initially the person rejected it out of hand. So advice-giving, I think, is a very important part of therapy and I will often be fairly free with my advice always phrasing it, 'This is the way I see it, this is my subjective opinion'. The advice is not given in a dictatorial sense. I might parenthetically say, that I feel that our state of knowledge is such that it is important for us to be humble and to state things tentatively. 'This is my subjective opinion, this is how I see it, according to my perceptions, so-and-so seems to be the case'. You see there's a difference between saying 'I think it would be a good idea if you chatted to your brother' and 'You must do that'. Let's avoid being presumptuous, or arrogant. So advice-giving is not instruction-giving; it's sharing an impression, a suggestion, a feeling and letting the person run with it and make a decision.

w.d.   One of the phrases you mentioned earlier was 'It depends', and I think you would be the first to caution against changing an absolute don't into an absolute do. Therefore, when would you not give a client advice?

a.l.   A very good point. Every do and don't can have its exceptions. At times I have given advice, and I have found that the person had distorted what I had said. For example I might have said, 'I think it would be a good idea if you thought of changing jobs in the near future'. And the person comes back and says, 'Last time you told me that I should go and have it out with my boss and really confront him'. These distortions need to be guarded against. When I discover that I am dealing with the kind of person who distorts and twists suggestions that I make, I become wary. When I make a recommendation, I ask the person to repeat back to me what I have just said. At other times, I question the person and say, 'What do you think might be a good way to proceed?' and let them put forth a *modus operandi*. So there is one example of when I modify advice-giving or decide not to give advice.

w.d.   Are there any other circumstances?

a.l.   Yes. Some clients approach you with a plan that they want to bounce off somebody without being told what you think, how you view it, or what they should do. They are really not interested in that, but want to hear themselves talk to somebody, and then go ahead and do what they want to do, and unless there are good reasons for them to act differently, you might simply listen and say, 'What you have told me is very interesting', and avoid any kind of advice-giving or suggestions.

w.d.   Let's go on to your next erroneous don't.

a.l.   The next unfortunate don't is *'Don't self-disclose'*. I have been told that it is very important for the therapist to be an enigma, to be detached, somewhat impersonal and impartial and if you self-disclose you destroy the anonymity, you become too real. The person can no longer see in you what he or she wants to see in you, because you have disabused them, by giving them the truth. Selective self-disclosure can be very helpful, and often by saying to somebody 'I have been there' or 'I have felt that' or 'Let me tell you what I do when I feel depressed or if I get anxious', this can be extremely humanizing and helpful to many people. Many have appreciated it greatly. The fact that the therapist is not playing the role of a god pretending to be perfect, but is willing to share shortcomings, limitations, fears and doubts that he or she has, will often break down barriers and enhance the development of trust. But let me emphasize that it can backfire with some people who wish to see the therapist as a model of complete adjustment. In my experience, such clients are in the minority. So selective self-disclosure can be very useful.

w.d.   Distinctions have been made in the literature between coping self-disclosure and mastery self-disclosure. What you seem to be advocating is coping self-disclosure where a therapist says 'Well, I have experienced similar difficulties to you in the past and this is how I personally overcame them', rather than mastery self-disclosure where a therapist says 'I have never had such a problem, because I have always believed this or I have always done that'.

A.L.   And it's also fine to say, 'I am still struggling with some of those myself, I haven't entirely resolved them'. Now as already mentioned, the trouble with giving mastery disclosures is that they imply that the therapist is some impeccable, immaculate being who is totally out of orbit, with whom the client cannot identify, and that's rather unfortunate.

Perhaps I ought to add a few don'ts to the two I started out with: 'Don't boast and brag about how wonderful you are, and don't blow your own horn too loudly'. It certainly is useful at times, I might add, to build the placebo affect by mentioning some of one's credentials and training, but not by bragging or boasting. Mastery is not a good way to get people to make changes because they get discouraged, since it implies that perfect solutions exist, whereas in fact we struggle along, but some of us muddle through life better than others. If one can give this anti-perfectionistic aura of people struggling along and coping it's far more realistic than a picture of total mastery.

W.D.   Now again adopting the principle of 'It depends', when might you not self-disclose to a client?

A.L.   When clients are just not interested. I don't self-disclose when after revealing something about myself, it does not prove helpful, the person does not use this in the way I intended, or when he or she is quite disinterested. Also I would not self-disclose if I have evidence that the person may tend to use it against me, or will undermine the therapy. If I say, 'I am still struggling with specific issues in my own marriage', and the person comes back to the next session and begins to nail me, and proceeds to say that I need therapy myself because I am just as badly off as he or she is, I would make a mental note not to use self-disclosure that displays my own shortcomings to this person. Those I think are the main occasions when I would eschew that sort of intervention.

W.D.   OK, let's have a look at the next fallacious don't on your list.

A.L.   The next don't is a big one, *'Don't socialize'*, in fact it was *'Never socialize with clients'*. 'Boundary' was a very big word that some of my supervisors employed, implying that if you went beyond the confines of the consulting room, you would undermine your power and your efficacy. The idea that you might in fact accept a dinner invitation to a client's home, the fact that you might invite a client to join you at a movie, was unthinkable and strongly proscribed. There are many therapists who operate under these very rigid rules. I have sometimes found that I have gained information at a dinner party, on a tennis court or while taking a walk with a client, that would never have come out in my consulting room. I am just sorry that I don't have the opportunity to spend more time observing my clients in their natural habitat as it were. It's a little artificial just seeing them within the confines of four walls. But I don't want the reader to get the wrong impression. I do *not* spend a lot of time socializing with my clients; this is something that has been very selective. I would say that out of thousands of clients I have treated, I may have socialized with a few dozen, which is not a very high percentage. When I have socialized, it's been because I have sensed that this would be advantageous and that there was no *a priori* reason not to do so.

w.d.   What therapeutic reasons have you had for socializing with your clients?

a.l.   I sensed for example with one man, that he believed that I considered myself superior to him, and that if push came to shove, I would not want to be in his company, outside of my office. As long as he was paying me money, I would put up with him. This was not verbalized, but seemed to come through in some subtle innuendoes. During a session he asked if my wife and I would like to come to his house for dinner, and he gave me a particular date. I immediately thanked him and accepted the invitation. I could see that he was very pleased that I hadn't given him the professional brush-off. And indeed going to his home turned the therapy around and it gave him a feeling of acceptance that was far greater than I could give him in a professional role. Later when I reciprocated and invited this man and his wife to our home for dinner, with some of our mutual friends, this meant a great deal to him. And he said, as therapy progressed, this was pivotal in his experience.

Similarly a woman who was in therapy with me because of certain feelings of inferiority nevertheless described herself as a good tennis player. I called her up one evening and explained that my wife and I played tennis with another couple, but the wife of the other man was unable to come, and asked her if she would fill in. This meant a tremendous amount to her, and these kinds of gestures facilitated what we were doing and accomplishing in therapy. Now again, I knew my customer, I didn't just randomly do this, but from what had happened in the therapy, I deduced that this would be positive. I have at times been wrong.

w.d. Let's talk about some of those times. What were the factors that led you to conclude that you were wrong?

a.l. Well, talking about tennis, on another occasion with a different person, when I had invited her to play tennis, she thought I was making an overture, and she thought that this was my way of trying to seduce her. In her mind, asking her to play tennis meant something else and that we would eventually end up in bed. This emerged in the session after I called her; she had declined to come to tennis and I noticed that she was different in that session, though I was pleased that she brought it up. She could have been scared right out of therapy. After mentioning these thoughts, I expressed my gratitude to her for sharing them, and assured her that this was not my agenda.

w.d. Since most instances of sex between therapists and clients occur between male therapists and female clients should male therapists be more circumspect, particularly with their female clients, about extending the boundaries of therapy into the area of socializing?

a.l. You have to be careful that you don't play into certain fantasies. One of my students is a young, extremely attractive male, and I caution him, more so than I would your average-looking individual, to beware of the fantasies that he can engender with gay men and with heterosexual female clients. Such a man inviting clients to have dinner with him, play tennis with him, or go to a movie with him, would carry a far greater risk than would be true of less good-looking clinicians. I think people have to know their reinforcement value and limitations and operate within those.

w.d. Let's go back to the man who said that socializing with you was a pivotal point in his therapy. What if he wanted to develop the friendship further and you didn't?

a.l. Yes, it could become a problem, but no more of a problem than somebody in therapy who decides that you are fantastic and wants to continue seeing you, while you want to terminate the therapy because you consider that you have done all you can for this person. It's a little bit more touchy outside the consulting room but again I would be inclined to be frank and to say to this person that in fact my social calendar is very full and although we could be good, casual friends, the demands of my job, family, writing, research, travels, lectures, would make another continuous on-going social interaction very difficult. So I would keep the social interaction on an occasional basis. I don't think the person would come away devastated or crushed, but it would pose a dilemma.

The opposite has happened, a couple of times, where lasting friendships did develop after therapy ended. But I have been rather cautious in these matters and that is why I have not fallen into the awkward situation you posed earlier.

w.d. When would you definitely not extend the relationship outside of the boundaries of therapy?

a.l. If I sensed that there were ulterior motives and if I felt that the kind of unhappy ending that you alluded to was likely to occur. It is not difficult to size most people up and deduce that they will escalate matters, seek more and more reassurance, and end up feeling rejected. In these cases you can hide behind the shibboleth that it is against the ethical rules to socialize, so the person doesn't feel so rejected.

I also would not socialize if I thought that there was some form of exploitation. Now this did happen on one occasion when I read the cues incorrectly. This very wealthy man, who was in therapy with me for some obsessive-compulsive problems, extended a dinner invitation and I accepted. Subsequently I realized that what had happened was that he had invited a number of people and had expected me to be the entertainer to enhance his social image. He wanted to display me like a trophy, that his friend was a well-known psychologist, a raconteur and the life-and-soul of the party (a mutual acquaintance had so characterized me). I was in rather a pensive mood that night and preferred to take a back seat and observe and discuss issues with one or two people in a quiet fashion. He came to the next session extremely annoyed with me for having let him down. In no uncertain terms he told me what a social dud I was. So you see by accepting his social invitation I had made an error. Sometimes, however, those mistakes can be brought back into the therapy and used to the advantage of the client.

w.d. In terms of countertransference, before extending the boundaries of therapy do you examine your own motives?

a.l. Yes, I think that what some call countertransference is important in this regard. Why do I do what I am doing? We need to examine what impact our personalities are having on others and we need to examine why we ourselves develop certain feelings or reactions to our clients. There have been occasions, however, when there has not been time to examine the countertransference. Somebody comes up with a suggestion, 'Why don't we take a walk instead of sitting in the office?', and you instantly see that this is some kind of test. To pass the test you must agree instantly. You

haven't had a chance to examine your own feelings and motivations; you are responding to the immediacy of the request, and
hope that you read the signals correctly.

w.d.   When you have had the opportunity to examine your own
motives, have you decided that your motives weren't as 'kosher', as
they should be, with the result that you decided not to extend the
boundaries?

a.l.   One case that comes to mind was when I was treating a
publisher and he had extended an invitation for me to come to a
party and I wanted very much to accept. But I had the time to think
about why I was so eager and soon saw that it was because it would
have given me a chance to meet some influential people who could
have furthered what I was doing, as far as certain writings were
concerned. I felt to myself that this was an unfair exploitation, and
that it would also, in a certain sense, make me beholden to this man
and weaken what was happening in our therapy. Here was a man of
enormous power who had no power over me up to that point. I was
purely his therapist and I declined because I thought that would
undermine what we were trying to do. So this was one fairly recent
case in point.

w.d.   Let's have a look at your next don't.

a.l.   The next unfortunate don't is 'Don't accept gifts from clients'. I
was on a panel with a psychoanalyst some years back in Arizona; a
member of the audience had asked about the accepting of gifts and
he had said that he never would accept gifts. What he would do,
would be to interpret what was happening: he would honour the
moment, but he would not accept the gift. Instead he would make
the person aware of their motivations, whatever they might be.
And humorously I said surely it depends on the gift. With tongue
in cheek I said if I was being offered a cheap tie I too would handle
it in that way, I would not accept it. I would examine the
motivation (by the way, we were addressing an audience of over
1,000 people). I went on to say that if the person was offering me a
Mercedes Benz I would accept it graciously and drive away in it.
When the laughter died down, I took a more serious position and
said, 'It depends'. When would and wouldn't one accept gifts?
There are some people that you know very well who would come
with gifts in the hope of owning you or feeding into some of their
paternal or maternal fantasies and it's not a good idea to go ahead
and play into this. You may want to point out to them what you
think is happening. But with most people who offer a little gift like
a tie at Christmas time, a nice pair of socks, a tee shirt or something

they might have picked up on vacation, there's no need to suspect ulterior motives. It's such an insult not to graciously say, 'Thank you very much, I appreciate that; how nice of you to think of me on your vacation. I am really touched. I look forward to wearing this.' End of story without any interpretation. But I had one client who started plying me with many small gifts and immediately we had to stop this, for obvious reasons, and examine what was happening. I had another client whom I knew to be at the time a compulsive shop-lifter who offered me the most magnificent sweater I have seen in years. I asked if she had paid for it. And she said, 'I cannot tell a lie, I stole it'. I said, 'Well, as much as it hurts me, I cannot accept stolen goods, but thank you for the thought: you and I have go to try and work on your moral hierarchy'.

w.d.   You joked that you would accept a valuable gift, and turn down a less valuable one, but in reality would you accept a gift that you considered was more than a token of appreciation?

a.l.   No, the truth is, if somebody offers a gift that is more than, as you say, a token, I think it would be a mistake to accept it, because I think that then one is beholden; it smacks of bribery and it would feel like a power play. Also there are some very interesting ethical issues that have been spelt out by the American Psychological Association. Somebody who is a shareholder of vast corporations offers to give the therapist a gift of 1,000 shares which could be worth 10,000 dollars in a year or two. It would be a big mistake to accept the offer. It runs counter to the ethics of the American Psychological Association. There are some definite rules and regulations to follow in this regard.

w.d.   Have you ever given gifts to clients?

a.l.   You know, I am sure I have, although offhand I cannot recollect any. I often give books to clients, if that can be said to be giving gifts. I give many of my self-help books to clients hoping that this will facilitate therapy.

w.d.   You don't charge them for the books?

a.l.   Right, I don't charge them. Suppose a client said to me he had to go to a very important dinner and needed to borrow a tie, I'm sure I'd let him borrow or keep one of my ties. I could see myself doing that, but offhand I don't know if I have actually given gifts other than books.

w.d.   Have you ever sent a client a Christmas or birthday card, which is in a sense a gift?

a.l.   Yes, I have done that on occasion. I have this one client who was very disturbed, a young woman who had been brutally raped

by her mother's brother when she was 9, and whose father had died
shortly before that, and who regarded me at the end of therapy as
her adopted father, sent me cards on Father's day and on my
birthday and, although I have not seen her in therapy now for a
good four or five years, I have noted her birthday in my diary and I
send her a birthday card, and I know it means a lot to her, and it is
always signed YAD, which means 'Your adopted dad'.

w.d.   Let's have a look at the next don't on your list.

a.l.   The next one is *'Don't challenge or confront patients'*.

w.d.   Now of course in some therapies like rational-emotive therapy
or Gestalt therapy that isn't a don't. So could we consider in what
way it was a don't as part of your training?

a.l.   It was part of my training because initially I was taught by
psychodynamic and Freudian practitioners to avoid any kind of
confrontation, and to be very sparse even with any interpretations.
However, there is something to be said against challenging or
confronting, when it is done without class. I have seen it carried out
in a brash and unfortunate manner, and the person can emerge
feeling attacked and hurt. The distinction that is so often drawn
between challenging a person's behaviour versus challenging the
person is important here. When you challenge a person's behaviour
and accept the person, he or she may well feel unconditional regard
as a human being, but when you challenge the person as a whole, he
or she may well feel put down by you. So challenging and
confronting must be done with finesse, with grace, or it can
backfire. But I don't think we have to dwell too much on that,
because there are many schools of thought today that don't, even
for a moment, subscribe to this particular don't.

w.d.   So let's move to your next unfortunate don't.

a.l.   The next don't I want to mention is somewhat tied into the one
about not accepting gifts, and it's *'Don't accept favours'*. A client
says something like, 'I will look up this reference for you and pop it
in the mail' or 'Why don't I give you a ride to pick up your car at the
service station: it is on my way'. My teachers would recommend
against accepting favours. Even worse would be for the therapist to
ask for a favour: 'I wonder if you would do me a favour, and mail
this letter for me, if you pass a mail box on the way home'. I was
told in my training days you must never do that. Now there is a fine
dividing line here, of course, between accepting small favours and
exploiting certain patients. Obviously I am against exploitation.
There are those who would argue that asking somebody to mail a
letter is exploitation. I think that's silly. If psychotherapy is

practised under the guise of some stylized professionalism, it becomes arid, dry, sterile and inhuman. But if we see therapy as involving human beings working together with a view to being helpful, solving problems and pooling resources, then there is more fluidity and freedom. Would I hesitate to say to a colleague, be a pal and mail this letter for me? No. Why would I then hesitate with a client? It's different, if the person says no, they are not going anywhere near a mail box, but they will drive four miles out of their way in the snow to mail this letter for me: that would be exploitation. So I say that part of being a human therapist is you can accept small favours and often make minor requests.

w.d.   Again have there been times when you have regretted doing so, when it has turned out to be a mistake?

a.l.   Yes. One of the problems about working the way I do is that I sometimes have regrets and there are times when I am well aware that Freudians and Rogerians never get into this kind of hot water.

w.d.   Partly because it seems as though you are prepared to take more risks?

a.l.   That's correct. I have been lucky that most of them have paid off, they have paid dividends, but there have been instances when I have regretted it. Some people can easily feel abused or taken advantage of. A client might say, 'You have a nerve asking me to drop a package off with my next-door neighbour. I am not a delivery boy. You can deliver it yourself.' This is an actual quote. What had happened in the session was the person had mentioned that he lived next door to certain people who were expecting a package from me, they were next-door neighbours. This had come out fortuitously, and I said, 'How funny, I have a package I am about to mail to them', and the client said, he would be glad to drop it off, since it's right next door. He actually made the offer. When I took him up on it and said that would be very kind of him, it would certainly speed things up, later in the session the client changed his mind and accused me of having a darn nerve.

w.d.   How did you respond?

a.l.   I responded by saying that the offer appeared to be a genuine offer, that it was perhaps a test which I failed. If I had passed the test I would have insisted on going to the Post Office myself. I also enquired whether he had changed his mind because he did not want his neighbours to find out that he was undergoing therapy. The client denied the latter but confirmed the former. So I pointed out that because he had made an offer that he wanted me to refuse, he was not being authentic with me. I said something like,

'I believed you, when you said it was no trouble, and accepted your kindness. On the other hand does this mean that this is how you are with other people as well, is this something you do? Do you perhaps set up other people in this fashion by tricking them in this way? You tricked me into accepting what I thought was a simple kind offer.' So I was able to get therapeutic mileage out of it.

w.d.   That leads us on to another viewpoint which I have heard stated quite frequently, namely that the way the client interacts with their therapist is somehow prototypical of the way that they react to other people in their social world. Does this notion have much validity or is it a sacred cow?

a.l.   I regard it as a sacred cow and think that it has to be checked out. In the foregoing example, we had a case in which I was asking, whether a prototypical pattern had emerged. One might ask, 'Is this person-specific or do you set up others similarly?' or 'Is this the only time this has happened in your life?' 'Is this the first time you have done such a thing?' or 'Is this something you do with most other people?' It turned out that in the foregoing case this was something he did frequently and that it was prototypical. But it doesn't have to be a general pattern. Of course we all have a fairly consistent way of responding when we feel cheated, or angry, or misunderstood, and so forth.

Clients who view you as a parent figure may be inclined to treat you or relate to you as they do to their parents. If they regard you as a policeman or an authority figure, then maybe they will relate to you as they would relate to a policeman or other figures. But they won't relate to you as they do to their friends or their siblings, because you are perceived in a different light. So you have to check the person's specific perceptions, feelings and apperceptions; it's of course not unreasonable to assume that people have a limited repertoire and the way they respond in the office to a given situation might very well be the same way that they would respond in a different setting. I remember a situation in which a student therapist was working under my supervision, and he made a remark that his client regarded as an ethnic slur. The client became enraged, and bellowed at the therapist. Now the question here was, is this how he would have responded to most people, or was there something about the student-therapist that was annoying him in particular? This needs to be checked out instead of automatically calling it 'negative transference'. It turned out that this man's volatile temper was one of his major problems. The way he blew up at the therapist was put to good effect in the therapy by showing this man that it is preferable to respond assertively by simply saying, 'Gee I feel that's an ethnic slur, that's a put-down, I find that a very distressing expression that you have used', and thus to deal with it in a civilized assertive fashion.

w.d.   Since we are discussing this issue, what is your position on the issue of transference in multimodal therapy?

a.l.   Transference has been written about extensively by psychoanalytic practitioners and is a vast and complex subject. Let's refer to a few basic observations. It is not difficult to see or understand that you can transfer your affections from one person to another, negatively and positively, that somebody may meet you as a therapist and feel very good about you, because perhaps you remind them of someone who was kind to them when they were little. A woman came and told me she was very nervous about her session, but the moment she saw me she was at ease because I reminded her very much of her father, with whom she had a good relationship. You see that's an example of so-called transference: 'He reminds me of my father; my father was good, so he will be good'. If the father had been nasty, this could have contaminated our relationship and she could have developed a negative transference. I think there's validity in those straightforward issues. We have all had the experience of disliking somebody intensely even though we don't know him or her, and if asked why, we would probably have to delve into our memories and dig up the fact that this person reminds us, looks like, acts like, moves like, somebody we have good reason to dislike from our past experiences. This is what learning theorists call stimulus generalization and response generalization. Working with a positive transference which, to my mind, translates into rapport, a good working relationship, a healthy liaison, tends to facilitate the goals of most therapists. Taking transference beyond that delimited meaning, as many theorists have done, I think just muddies the waters. Once we start talking about repressed, unconscious, conflictual childhood memories or reliving deeply held infantile desires, we enter the quagmire of psychoanalytic speculations.

w.d.   Many theoreticians and practitioners regard the relationship between the therapist and the client as the prime vehicle for change. True or sacred cow?

a.l.   The relationship is the context that allows change to occur and is sometimes necessary and sufficient; often times it is necessary but insufficient. If you have a patient, who has a bipolar disorder and is in a manic phase, it matters little how good the relationship is, the chances are that this person will continue to suffer until treated with the right medication, which is lithium.

W.D.   But if you have a good relationship with such clients this may encourage them to take their medication.

A.L.   Correct, but you cannot ascribe the change to the relationship. The relationship will foster the technique. If you have a good relationship, you might be able to encourage phobic patients to expose themselves to their feared situations thereby mitigating the phobias, you might encourage obsessives or compulsives to stop their rituals thereby producing an attenuation of their habit patterns, you may be able to persuade the unassertive person to take risks, so yes, the relationship is necessary but insufficient. But again I have to say that there are so many conditions where the most empathic wonderful understanding relationship will not produce change of any significance, unless within that context of a good relationship the proper techniques are correctly applied.

|6| TRAINING AND SUPERVISION

WINDY DRYDEN   I would now like to focus on your views concerning training and supervising therapists. But first I would like to ask you what qualities good multimodal therapists should demonstrate, since this probably underpins your view on training and supervision?

ARNOLD LAZARUS   Good multimodal therapists are flexible, and have a broad array of techniques at their disposal. They can talk in a concise and accurate fashion, they are perceptive and sensitive to relevant and highly charged emotional issues. They display profound respect and significant understanding and they use humour appropriately in their sessions. I would say that their major facilitative conditions include empathy, respect, genuineness, warmth, concreteness, appropriate self-disclosure and immediacy. Whether or not one can train people to develop these core qualities is an important question. Personally I think that these attributes are there to begin with and that if they are not evident by the time a person is plus or minus 14 years, they will not develop. Those that do not possess them to start with, I think will end up without them, regardless of their academic credentials or the excellence of a clinical training programme to which they are exposed.

w.d.   In this respect, if you had to pick one quality above all, what would it be?

a.l.   I would say that it's a combination of someone who is truly non-judgemental and has a wide range of skills. So it's a highly skilled non-judgemental individual. That would be the crux for me.

w.d.   How do you assess whether or not a person applying to you for training has such qualities?

a.l.   The entire problem of student selection remains enigmatic.

We have a programme at Rutgers University in which some 400 people apply for the clinical PsyD degree (Doctor of Psychology Degree in Clinical Psychology) and we select about fifteen or sixteen people. The ratio who are selected into the clinical PhD programme is even more stringent. And yet invariably year after year we find that we have made some poor choices; we have selected less than desirable people, some of whom have to be let go. After scrupulously looking through letters of recommendation, grades, autobiographical statements, interviewing the students, having two, three or four faculty people come up with independent evaluations, you would think that we would be able to screen them, so that unpleasant and noxious trainees would be excluded. I suppose it is true that relatively speaking, most of our students turn out to be fine people and good clinicians, but why a few 'losers' manage to slip through that fine mesh remains a mystery. Of course our evaluation and assessment techniques are anything but perfect.

However, when I get to choose a multimodal trainee the person has already been through the general selection process, has been in one or two of my formal classes and supervision groups, and I have got to know this person pretty well. Often I have interacted with him or her socially and had a chance to see interactions with several other people, and have received the impressions of a wide range of their peers and my colleagues. Thus there are a lot of data there by the time I get round to choosing somebody to train specifically in multimodal work. I am accused sometimes of being an elitist because I am so particular in whom I choose in this regard, and I have to plead guilty as charged. But I think it is important to try and find the right people to do this job correctly.

w.d.   What training activities would you say are particularly useful in helping trainees to develop skills and broaden repertoires?

a.l.   To me, the apprenticeship model is the most powerful, which means the student clinician does therapy and receives supervision in which he or she can discuss exactly what is happening. Their trainers have opportunities to listen to them on audiotapes, observe videotapes and sometimes watch behind a one-way mirror. The trainees also observe experienced therapists in action and serve as co-therapists. They get lots of feedback.

Now let me say a word or two about giving feedback. I am put out by some of my fellow supervisors and trainers who tell the students that they have made serious mistakes. They will say something like, 'You shouldn't have suggested that the patient change jobs until you had interviewed him four times', or they will say, 'It was a mistake for you to have suggested that he has this discussion with his uncle at that time'. And I ask, 'How can you be so sure, whether it was a mistake or whether in fact it turns out to be excellent timing?' I prefer to say to my students, 'Let's think of options. What you did was one option, but could there have been something better?' I encourage them to consider many different options. Breadth is a very important concept to me. So thinking of options opens and expands minds, and it's a much better way of training people than to say this was right, this was wrong, because by doing so, one is putting oneself in a superior position and often I think, calling the shots incorrectly.

w.d.   Taking the apprenticeship model, have you found that instead of developing their own skills, trainees tend to model themselves on you and try to be a carbon copy of you?

a.l.   I have made that criticism of some eminent therapists, most notably Albert Ellis, where I have noticed that so many of the people who work for him, end up trying to emulate him, even down to his Bronx accent and even copy his non-verbal gestures. Ellis's trainees try and use his language form and his expressions, but they are pale effigies of the master, instead of being their own people. Being aware of this phenomenon, I guard against it with my own students and if I feel that they are trying to put on something that doesn't fit them, I encourage them to adapt it to their own way in their own style and to be their own people. In the area of training when I refer to an apprenticeship, I am not thinking of a master–apprentice relationship, a pure one on one, as much as having a number of different people that one would work under: several role-models. So that a lot of the students who get trained by me also spend time with other supervisors, who are *au fait* with multimodal methods and they observe other multimodal clinicians in action. But they are encouraged always to be themselves.

w.d.   With respect to supervision, how important is it for you to hear what trainees have actually done (on audiotape, for example) rather than to work with their reports about what they have done?

a.l.   It gets a little cumbersome for some people to record every session and some clients feel a little put out by this, so I don't have any rigid rules. But I do from time to time like to obtain a tape to note the difference between what they have said they have done, and what they have actually done, and to form my impressions of what I have heard on the tape. Again feedback is given in terms of 'Here is something that you might have done there' or 'Did you consider that?' I like to ask the student why he or she took one position rather than another. So that the individual comes to realize that we always have these options and that we make choices. A way that I train students quite often is by playing them tapes of sessions either of other students or of my own sessions. I stop the tape at a specific point and ask for suggestions about effective ways of proceeding, and then we listen to what actually happened on the tape. I like to talk about response couplets. This means that if the patient responds, you the therapist also have got to respond. The patient says 'Should I go into town today?' The therapist now has to respond. The therapist can do so by just looking at the patient while saying nothing, the therapist can say 'Mm, mmh', the therapist can rephrase the question, but the therapist must respond: there is no way out. And then you try and rate the response in terms of its facilitative impact and talk about what other responses were possible and might have proved more effective. So using response couplets in training has been a valuable procedure that I have used.

w.d.   In your approach to training and supervision, you seem then to try and broaden the range of your trainee therapists' responses and to encourage them to think for themselves.

a.l.   That's very well put.

w.d.   In your experience, how important is it to recommend your trainee therapists to have their own personal therapy?

a.l.   I don't think that personal therapy is necessary unless there is evidence that the trainee has problems that are getting in the way, compromising his or her clinical effectiveness. The old cliché is if it's not broken, don't fix it. There are those who feel that personal therapy is a *sine qua non*; admission to certain professional organizations is contingent upon the clinician having had a number of hours of personal therapy. I have written letters to some of these organizations asking whether this implies that everybody who enters our field is disturbed and should have therapy. What about healthy, well-functioning individuals who become therapists and don't need therapy, do such people exist? But they have not answered me satisfactorily. There are times when my trainees have said that they desire to have therapy for various reasons and there have been other times when I have noted that they may need therapy. Most recently I noticed that one of my trainees was using a good deal of self-disclosure and I inquired why he had elected to talk about various topics: was it for his own benefit or did it really help the client? At first he insisted that his revelations were all intended to be beneficial for the client, but as we discussed it further, he began to see that he was getting some free therapy from the client and this had happened once or twice too often. I pointed out that he seemed to have some issues that he may want to talk to a professional about, and recommended that he do so, which he followed through on. There was another trainee who tended to be very defensive and I felt that if she were on the receiving end of antagonism from a patient she would not be non-judgemental and open, she would immediately counterattack and defend. I shared this observation with her and suggested that therapy might help her feel more secure and less defensive, thereby making her a better clinician. So those are a few specific cases. But on the whole, I don't believe that it is necessary for everybody who practises psychotherapy to have been in therapy.

w.d.   Let's suppose that somebody in their late teens or early twenties came to you and said that in ten years' time, he or she wanted to train as a therapist. How would you recommend that that person spend the next decade, experiencing life before entering psychotherapy training?

a.l.   What I think is important is for people to know who and what is out there. For example I think that somebody who grows up in a very affluent environment, a bright kid who goes to high school and university and has an easy life, is smart, gets good grades, and socializes with the upper crust, and then proceeds to open up an office having obtained a degree in psychiatry or psychology, would probably be an ineffective therapist by virtue of not knowing who or what is out there. This person may possess insufficient empathy due to limited life experience. So I would advise this person to associate with a wide range of people drawn from different ethnic and socio-economic backgrounds, to be able to know what the world is made up of. I think back to some of the things that have helped me do effective therapy. These add up to a variety of experiences I had when I was selling houses, working in a department store as a kid, travelling to different places, spending time on a farm and seeing how differently the farm kids interacted from the urban kids with whom I had socialized all the time. I attended several different high schools, which in retrospect turned out to be a good thing. It taught me about diversity and I think that acquiring a first-hand knowledge of vast individual differences prevented me from going into a narrow mould which so many of my colleagues seem to prefer. Now I advise would-be clinical psychology trainees to consider taking an extensive course in writing and literary criticism in order to acquire the capacity to be able to express oneself succinctly and accurately. This is very important because words are the tools that we use most of the time and if we are unable to articulate clearly what it is that we want to convey, it's like a surgeon operating with blunt scalpels. People taking courses in method acting may enhance the use of techniques like role-playing and rehearsal procedures. So get breadth, young man or woman, would be the basic message that I would give to them.

w.d. Do you think that there are minimum and maximum ages when selecting trainees for multimodal therapy?

a.l. I am a little distressed when I find that some bright young person who finished high school at 14 or 15 and is now all of about 19 or 20 is admitted into the doctoral programme. With such minimal life experience, having been on this planet for a mere two decades, I feel that it is premature. If I had my way, I would not have people admitted into doctoral training until they had been around for a quarter of a century. If they start their doctoral studies at age 25 or so by the time they are licensed and ready to work, they would be about 30. This would be a reasonable time trajectory that makes sense given normal life expectancy.

w.d. What about the maximum?

a.l. It depends on the individual. We have had students in our programme in their fifties, and these individuals brought maturity and experience to their studies. We have had people come into our programme who have been lawyers, dentists, engineers or successful business executives who decided they wanted to get into clinical psychology. Personally I have found, with few exceptions, that it is rather refreshing to train mature and seasoned students, as opposed to youngsters who are still wet behind the ears, as the saying goes. I know there is a cut-off point in this country [USA] in most medical schools. Some medical schools will not accept anyone, if I am not mistaken, who is more than in their mid-thirties. To think of having somebody start medical school in their fifties would not be viewed favourably. But I don't think that one ought to have age discrimination; it depends so much on the individual.

w.d. I know you have had some experience of training people in multimodal therapy who were originally trained in other therapy orientations. Has their prior training been either a help or a hindrance when it comes to learning the multimodal approach to psychotherapy?

a.l. It depends how disenchanted they are with their previous training. I had a psychiatrist who asked for training in multimodal therapy, after serving as the chief resident at a psychoanalytic institute. He had been thoroughly schooled in psychoanalytic principles and procedures, but had independently become incredibly disenchanted with this orientation and it was a pleasure working with him. He was bright and capable and he certainly did not hang on to any of his residual psychodynamic stereotypes. But I have had other people who have come and asked me for training but who could not relinquish the analytic tradition and remained very committed to it. In these instances, I've found it a definite hindrance where, from my viewpoint, instead of dealing with certain obvious issues, there was a penchant for the person to get into putative motives in much greater detail than seemed to be warranted. I have had other people who have come for training in multimodal therapy who have been 'retreaded', I think this is the word that is used. They may have been first trained as experimental, developmental or educational psychologists and then underwent a two-and-a-half-year programme and obtained clinical training and an internship and then asked for additional training in multimodal therapy. I have had varied results with them. These are different from the people that I referred to earlier who get selected into our programme and with whom I work closely and intensely for a number of years.

I have colleagues who started out as students, working closely with me for four or five years, who then have done post-doctoral training under my direct supervision, and who then formed ongoing continuing education seminars. We have ongoing meetings where we all manage to learn from one another.

w.d.   Because multimodal therapy rests, as we said earlier, on social learning theory, would you anticipate that people coming from a behavioural or cognitive-behavioural training background would make more natural multimodal therapists than people who come from a different theoretical background?

A.L.   Relatively speaking we get far fewer requests for serious training in multimodal therapy from people who are steeped in dynamic theories or existential theories. The majority of people have been of a behavioural persuasion with one or two exceptions.

w.d.   How important do you think it is for a trainee therapist to have had experience of personal pain or distress and to have had the experience of knowing what it is like to have been in the client role, prior to training?

A.L.   Quite important. I referred earlier to the worst kind of training background being the affluent individual who has sailed through life and breezed through situations effortlessly. I think they make the worst therapists because empathy comes from suffering, and if one has not oneself experienced psychological pain, it's very hard, if not impossible, to understand what the other person, the client, is going through, and consumers will usually·pick this up. I would say that the best trainees are the ones who, as you say, have been hurting at one time but who are hurting a lot less now, because they have found either through personal therapy or their own life experiences, a way around the pain or through the pain. But receiving therapy just to be in the client role is not something that I would endorse.

w.d.   If you could offer one major warning to trainees from both within and outside your own tradition, what would that be?

a.l.   The major warning that I would want to offer is that the outcome literature suggests that a fair percentage of clients get over their problems without therapy, that there are some problems that are self-limiting. Some people get depressed: it lasts for a few months and they get over it. Some people are anxious or conflicted or stressed out and they overcome it spontaneously. Meanwhile, if they have entered therapy and the therapist has been using his or her favourite strategies and the person gets better, the therapist falls into the superstitious trap of believing that his or her ministrations were the agents of change, whereas they could in fact have had nothing to do with the improvements. It seems to be an unfortunate fact that anybody can invent a form of therapy. You and I right now could make up a form of therapy which could consist of staring into a tea cup, followed by a meditation mantra, topped off by rhythmic breathing, and everybody whom we saw could be given the tea cup, meditation and breathing strategy. A fair number of people would go away saying, 'This was wonderful! It was most relaxing and uplifting and I feel great.' If we really believed that our silly procedures were truly responsible that would be unfortunate. A therapist can be pretty inexperienced, inadequate and ineffective and still get about a 40 per cent remission rate unless he or she works with very difficult clients, in which case the percentage would be less. So the warning we must heed is to accept the null hypothesis that suggests that, in all probability, what we think was responsible for the change, probably had little to do with it.

I cannot overstate the need for humility in this field. For people to be cocksure that they have the answers is a terrible trap to fall into. It's so easy for therapists to develop superstitions because of this fairly high spontaneous remission rate. Your common-or-garden variety neurotic will respond to a touch of empathy, warmth and kindness from anyone; if a therapist, in addition to offering the kindness that is required, has a special technique that he delivers, and ascribes all the power and the credit to that, it is very misleading. It would be like a doctor believing in the power of carrot juice, but prescribing an antibiotic for a strep throat and then insisting that the patient drink the antibiotic with carrot juice, and giving all the credit to the carrot juice. So we must not forget that about half the neurotics of this world get better with or without treatment, and therefore we must try to make sure that we are using strategies of proven effectiveness because it is so easy to fall into the trap of believing in specious, spurious and irrelevant realities.

w.d.   That's a good warning for people who are trained as well as those in training.

a.l.   Yes, Windy, I think it's important.

w.d.   What advice would you give a trained multimodal therapist concerning seeking further training and supervision?

a.l.   It's interesting to use the expression 'trained' as though there is an end point, a final set of criteria that constitutes a fully trained individual. As you and I have discussed in another context, one is never fully trained because we don't have enough knowledge for any of us to be 'trained', so we are always *in training*. I guess this is why we are also in practice. We are trying to improve what we are doing. It would be unfortunate if anybody set himself or herself up in a position of such awesome knowledge and authority as to require no input from others.

Speaking personally, I do not hesitate to discuss difficult clients with professional friends and colleagues, and also with my students. I believe that two heads are better than one and often by bouncing around vignettes and ideas with somebody who is bright, you can learn, no matter who you may be.

w.d.   Do you only do that when you are experiencing problems with clients, or do you also do it when you sense you could intervene more effectively than you are presently doing?

a.l.   I probably ask for help or input from others mainly when I run into barriers or obstacles, or when I feel out of my depth. If things are going along smoothly, why bother, but if there are some problems that make you feel lost or bewildered, or when you feel that you are doing OK, but you could do better, why not bring it to the attention of somebody else, and discuss the issues? As I said, I have done that very often to good effect.

w.d.   What about extramural training activities? Since you are now talking personally, to what extent do you attend workshops, run by others, or seek training from others who might extend your own practice?

a.l.   Truthfully not as much as I would like to, mainly due to laziness, but I do get to a number of workshops each year, and I find it very fascinating to watch other therapists in action. I almost always come away with an extra tip or two, a new idea or two. I think that ongoing continuing education is very necessary. Of course some states mandate this; if you do not attend a certain number of credit hours you may lose your licence, and I think that is probably a good thing.

w.d.   Do you personally learn these tips from reading other people's work, or do you think it is more important to attend the workshops and see them in action?

a.l.   Personally I get a lot out of reading, but I have colleagues who tell me that they are very visual, and if they don't see it happening, if they just read about it, it doesn't have the same impact on them. But as I said, for me reading has been a very important training medium, but I do also like buying cassette tapes of various clinicians in action.

w.d.   In the last five years who and what has influenced you most in helping you to develop your own work?

a.l.   I have very useful discussions, lots of 'shop talk', with my good friend and colleague Allen Fay, who is a psychiatrist with a penchant for attending lots of workshops and a most gifted and brilliant clinician. He has described many of his own interventions, as well as the important things that he has learnt from workshops, and this has been very enriching. Watching Allen during therapy and doing co-therapy with him has also been a learning experience. Discussions with my colleague G.T. Wilson, who is a very prominent professor at Rutgers University and a brilliant researcher and scholar, has also proved to be extremely useful. Discussions with other colleagues – Cyril Franks for instance – have been most educational and debates with Stanley Messer have proved illuminating. Several of my post-doctoral students have made me aware of new information, and interactions with Albert Ellis have been a source of great inspiration over the last twenty years. And last but not least I have gained a lot from our tape correspondence over the last five or so years.

   I find that some of the writings of David Barlow in recent years, his book on *Anxiety and its Disorders* (Barlow 1988) for instance, has been most informative. Barlow has explicated some of the most important strategies for dealing with panic disorders, anxiety disorders, phobic disorders and compulsive disorders; after reading his material, my clinical repertoire was enhanced and enriched. My attendance at certain workshops at the Society for the Exploration of Psychotherapy Integration (SEPI) has also proved very useful in the past five years.

w.d.   Does anybody stand out in particular from SEPI?

a.l.   Yes, some of the people with whom I disagreed, for example Sam and Diana Kirschner, who are family systems therapists and who believe that therapy is always reparenting, a view that I strongly disagree with. My debates with them have been most stimulating. I learn a good deal from informal get-togethers with colleagues over lunch or dinner. I have also attended a number of meetings of the American Psychological Association and the Association for Advancement of Behavior Therapy and observed clinicians demonstrating procedures. Neil Jacobson is someone who has enhanced my marriage therapy repertoire at these meetings. So those are some of the main people and experiences over the past four or five years that have been especially helpful.

7

A POT-POURRI OF
THERAPEUTIC ISSUES

WINDY DRYDEN   I now want to discuss a number of issues, some of which people have suggested that I put to you. So to start with, do you ever see friends, family members or colleagues as clients in therapy?

ARNOLD LAZARUS   I am aware that there are some clinicians who contend that to treat family members or friends borders on unethical practice and is certainly ill advised. I come back with my usual retort: 'It depends'. So clearly the answer is yes, there have been times that I have treated friends and family members. In one instance some close friends of ours were having marital distress and after seeing several therapists asked me if I would see them professionally. I was reluctant to do so. They were insistent and proclaimed that we should at least give it a shot, since they knew me, and had confidence in me. They were also adamant that this should be treated truly professionally, that they would pay my fee and obtain their insurance reimbursements and we'd go about this thing in a strictly professional fashion. That's the only time there has been something quite that formal. In other instances when I say I have treated friends and family members, I mean, we have sat down as friends and I have been a therapist, and we have had a 'session', but money has not changed hands. It's been informal treatment.

W.D.   And where you both have not agreed that this is a therapy session?

A.L.   Well, it was designated as such. Friends or family members have said, 'I need some therapy', and we have gone into my office, sat down for an hour and chatted. They often wanted to pay me and, of course, I have refused. In my book friends don't accept money from friends, but occasionally I might have been given a gift. So I haven't got any hard and fast boundaries around this issue. Many years ago, one of my sisters had quite a number of extensive discussions with me that added up to 'therapy'. The way I dealt with her was very similar to what I would have done if she had been a genuine fee-paying client. Although she happened to be my sister, I think that she was assisted in achieving what she needed to do in several important areas of her life.

w.d.   Where do you draw the professional line on this issue?

a.l.   Well, again it would depend upon the problem and the individual. I would not want to see friends or family members with really serious dysfunctions. Certainly if I had *a priori* evidence that our relationship would suffer if I 'played therapist', I would demur. Not too long ago, a friend had asked me if I would chat with him about some of his difficulties which I agreed to do. When he recommended that I meet with him and his wife, I drew the line, because I had reason to believe that his wife would play one against the other, and this would be most unfortunate, because our friendship could be undermined. I expressed this to him and he saw what I was saying and I referred them to a colleague for the rest of the 'therapy'.

w.d.   Have you ever regretted seeing a friend, family member or colleague in therapy?

a.l.   Well, I treated a former student who has a private practice and I sure regretted it. He turned out to be extremely paranoid, hostile, accusatory and threatening. This could happen with any profoundly disturbed client. The fact that he was a former student and then a colleague was perhaps incidental. But this did not turn out well.

I remember treating a colleague with a penchant to become irrationally angry about minor infractions or alleged slights, from whom I received a very angry letter that was completely off the wall, attacking me for some putative oversight. Now again, the fact that he happened to be a colleague was perhaps irrelevant. All clinicians receive these distorted negative reactions from some people. So I am saying that I have had negative reactions when treating some colleagues, but it had more to do with who and what they were as people.

w.d.   What do you think of the traditional view of this issue, which states that it is not wise to see friends, family members or colleagues as clients, because if there are any difficulties arising out of the therapy it would then affect the relationship that existed prior to therapy.

a.l.   Again I would come back to the 'It depends' statement. If I sensed that what we were doing could compromise our friendship in some way, or if the friendship itself would undermine what I would want to do to be helpful, I would make a referral to some impartial outsider.

w.d.   Again a more traditional therapist might say 'But even if at this point I can predict that it won't happen, there is always a chance of it happening, and thus I am not prepared to take the risk'. It seems as if on this issue, as on others, you are more of a risk-taker than more traditional therapists.

a.l.   Yes, many people prefer to play it safe, to take few risks of any kind. I think what we are picking up here is that I don't endorse rigid lines of demarcation. I see life, therapy, friendships, interactions and discussions as part of a continuum. When you describe me as a risk-taker, I suppose this is true, but I would argue that I am not an irresponsible risk-taker, I am not a thrill-seeker, who does silly things simply to defy the authorities. But I see other people as having these definite categories. They say, 'I wear my professional hat and I wear my social hat, and I wear my parental hat', and so forth. I am distressed by these rigidities. But the point that you have made is well taken.

So let us examine when might one say to a family member, let's do some therapy, and when wouldn't one? Well, clearly as I have already said, if the situation is serious – and by serious I mean that the person is suffering from very definite psychopathology – I think it is far better to have an outside professional, because it is very hard to maintain a sense of objectivity when dealing with an extremely serious issue in someone close to you. So the therapy that I have done with friends and family, and so on, has not focused on significant deep-seated problems. Rather it has been on simple marriage difficulties, matters of interpersonal style, job-related problems, and on issues involving daily stress. To be able to say to a loved one, 'I as a professional have a repertoire of strategies that I can share with you that you can try on for size', makes eminent sense to me. People who would withhold that kind of kindness from their loved ones are a bit strange, in my opinion.

w.d.   So you have two major criteria in mind. The first one is your assessment of the severity of the person's problem. Here the more severe the problem, the more likely you are to suggest to the person that he or she sees somebody else. Second, you are not likely to take on someone you know for therapy if doing so might negatively affect the relationship you already have with them, and will have with them again after therapy is finished.

A.L. You have summarized it very well. I am thinking of three people I know, with whom I am friendly, but who I would not even dream of accepting as clients formally or informally, and the reasons are different for each one. One case is a lady who tends to mind-read. I have noticed this in social situations and by mind-reading I mean she will end up telling other people what they are thinking and feeling and will not take 'No' for an answer. I would not want to get involved with her in any clinical capacity, because I would see that process as deleterious. So she is fine and entertaining for my wife and I to have dinner with, when her husband and she are around, but that's it, that's the full extent of it.

The second instance concerns a man with whom I play tennis on occasion, who is a fine tennis partner, and also as a buddy with whom to sling back a beer or two afterwards. But there is something about his passive-aggressive style that would make any more intimate contact quite unpleasant for me. If he approached me for therapy, or anything more intimate than we have, a closer friendship, I would be sure to say 'No'.

And the third person that pops into mind is a woman who is, let's say 'hysterical' by nature. While her histrionics are quite entertaining at times in social situations and she can be the life-and-soul of the party, I have a sense that if one became involved with her on a more fundamental level, this would militate against any therapeutic goals. If this woman asked me to refer her to a therapist, I would hesitate to provide the name of a good colleague or friend of mine because I would be rendering that person a disservice. This would not be an easy client. So these are just a few off-the-top examples of where I would certainly not plunge in and take the risk.

W.D. Moving on to a different question, how useful do you find diagnostic category systems like DSM-III-R.

A.L. I use them mainly for insurance purposes, because if you don't give DSM-III-R category or some such label, you don't get reimbursed. The vast majority of my clients are simply given the 300.02 label, which is a generalized anxiety disorder, a catch-all phrase.

Now, it is important to separate neuroses and psychoses, although the term 'neuroses' is no longer in vogue. For example if someone is diagnosed as schizophrenic and the diagnosis is based on evidence of florid hallucinations, delusions and other severe symptoms, it usually points up the need for medication and the availability of well-informed clinical help.

If one just looks through some of the diagnostic labels, there is value in knowing that somebody is suffering from, let's say, dementia, developmental disorders, various disruptive behaviour disorders, eating disorders, bipolar depressive reactions, and so forth. In such instances these labels mean something. If somebody says that this is a delusional paranoid disorder, one has a very good idea of what to expect. Likewise, with specific substance abuse you are getting some clues as to what the major issues are likely to be. When one is told that a client has a panic disorder, or suffers from agoraphobia without panic, you have a pretty good idea of what you are likely to find. But to use a DSM-III-R category such as a 'social phobia' does not tell you enough. In my terms you need a BASIC I.D. assessment to really round it out and see exactly where you are going to intervene, and what goals you need to establish. So some of the labels give you an overall clue, but not terribly much information of how you would proceed clinically. It can be meaningful to describe someone as having a hypo-active sexual desire disorder, or to say that a woman is anorgasmic, or that a man is troubled by premature ejaculation or, as it is called these days, rapid ejaculation. These categories can be quite helpful if one wants a general idea of what is happening. If someone says, 'This person has an adjustment disorder, with anxious mood or depressed mood or with physical complaints', you can infer that there have probably been environmental shifts, and that the ensuing problems are of a temporary nature. So there are some things to be gained.

w.d.   Several books have recently been published which use DSM-III-R to help develop treatment plans. What do you think of the trend of differential treatment based on differential diagnosis?

a.l.   I am a little wary of that trend because I prefer differential diagnosis to mean a BASIC I.D. assessment, which gives a more precise and clearer handle on where to intervene. So to specify that patients with an adjustment disorder with mixed emotional features require specific treatments of choice, would not mean the same to me as those people's BASIC I.D.s which would suggest a wide, interrelated array of interventions that might be most applicable.

w.d.   Summing up, would it be true to say that with some diagnostic categories you have a clearer idea of treatment approaches that you might use than with others. But in no case would a diagnostic category suggest a detailed treatment plan because you want to do your own more individualistic multimodal assessment which would suggest a more idiosyncratic treatment programme for a given individual.

A.L. That's absolutely right.

W.D. I want now to focus on the interface between the therapeutic and the biological domains in psychotherapy and ask your views on that interface and how closely you work with biologically oriented psychiatrists?

A.L. Well, as I have implied throughout our discussion, and I have also written this in many places, when treating someone with a condition like bipolar disorder, I think it borders on malpractice if you don't make sure that the person is put on lithium or some other kind of medication in addition to the other things that one would do multimodally with this person. The same would be true if somebody has florid hallucinations: they would probably need some phenothiazine derivative that a psychiatrist would monitor. I have close bonds with psychiatrists in the community who do the prescribing and attend to the medical aspects. While I work on, you might say, the 'BASIC I.', they attend to the 'D.', the biological modality.

W.D. One of the issues that we have been discussing throughout the book concerns how important it is to carry out a very sensitive detailed assessment across modalities. When it comes to the biological modality do you find that some psychiatrists carry out a very general non-individualistic assessment of the client's problems and offer medication based on that general assessment, whereas others are really tuned into the nuances of a person's biological system and can therefore tailor a particular 'cocktail' that would suit this particular person?

A.L. As in any other professional sphere, the range of knowledge and skill varies enormously from psychiatrist to psychiatrist, and indeed I know some who are abysmally ignorant and prescribe the wrong medications, often pick up incorrect clinical clues and make false diagnoses. What I have tried to find are very sharp, enlightened, astute biologically oriented psychiatrists, who indeed know what to prescribe, who monitor the patients carefully, who are well aware of the fact that the entire 'cure' does not come out of a bottle, and who appreciate the services that psychologists can provide. Some psychiatrists prefer doing psychotherapy and will use medications as they see fit. But I find it better to work with those psychiatrists who prefer not to do psychotherapy, but who specialize in drug therapy. In many instances I think that specific medications are vital. I found myself on a panel some years ago with a psychiatrist who was violently opposed to medication. His platform is that medication of any kind in psychiatry is unconscionable, since these are 'dirty drugs', meaning they have untoward side-effects; but he is an extremist, and it was very funny that I, a psychologist, ended up defending the use of medication against the psychiatrist, who was taking the position that some non-medical people take, totally condemning psychiatric drugs. As I said, I think that for some individuals specific medications are vital. People with certain kinds of depression, whose mood swings from high to low for no apparent reason, with severe anxiety, and especially persons who are prone to repeated breakdowns in which very irrational thoughts and feelings seem to be racing out of control, these are the people who benefit greatly from the proper use of psychiatric drugs in addition to the BASIC I. procedures that we have alluded to.

Medication is no substitute for learning new thinking and behaviour, although some people will feel remarkably better with the right drug. I always tell my patients when I refer them to a biological psychiatrist to make sure to inform the doctor whether a particular drug is helping or not. I tell them to ascertain the name of the drug prescribed, the recommended dose and its possible side-effects. The consumers need to be enlightened as to the reasons a drug is being prescribed. Now, some people mistakenly feel that medication is a crutch and they want to be independent, and do it on their own. It's no more of a crutch to take psychiatric medication than it is to wear glasses when you have difficulty seeing or to take allergy pills when you are suffering miserably from hay fever. Of course, one would want to caution people not to make the opposite error, that is of popping pills indiscriminantly as if they were answers to problems. But I find that some people don't like taking medication, because they see it as giving up control. Whereas quite the contrary, I think the availability of medication gives the sufferer the power to control whatever chemical factors may be contributing to his or her difficulty. So I think it is the wise person who knows how to use the resources of the environment to better himself or herself and promote well-being and happiness.

w.d.   Looking back over your career as a psychotherapist, is there one piece of work with a client which has given you particular satisfaction and one piece which has left you with the most regrets?

A.L.   I always have tremendous difficulty in zeroing in on 'ones'. If someone asks me to name my favourite food or favourite fruit or favourite book, I can never answer this. I can talk in plurals – about several favourite items. It is very hard for me to think back to one particular item or event that really stands out; I can think of some instances where I was tremendously gratified at the progress that people made, and how happy I was that coincidentally or otherwise after seeing me, their lives had changed. I can think of a number of these people. And I can also think of the tremendous frustrations I have experienced when I have failed miserably to be of service to some individuals, despite my most ardent and willing efforts. But to pick one piece of work is impossible for me.

w.d.   OK, but over the last year, can you think of one case where you felt that you did a good job, and one where you were disappointed with the way things turned out?

a.l.   May I start with the latter, the one that didn't go so well? This is someone I had treated about a year ago. After that I will tell you about another that did go well. We will start with the negative and end with the positive.

A couple that I was seeing were quite remarkable. The husband, a surgeon in his mid-thirties, and the wife, a lawyer of 32, were not getting along. The thing that struck me about this couple was how extraordinarily good-looking they were. They both looked as though they could go to Hollywood and become matinée idols. So here were these extremely attractive young professionals: the surgeon husband was a full partner in a large practice making inordinate amounts of money and his wife, the young lawyer, worked for a firm where she too made lots of money, and they had a delightful 2½-year-old daughter. The wife had said to me that in high school and college all her friends had identity crises, they didn't know what they wanted to be and do when they grew up. She had no identity crisis. She knew exactly what she wanted to do. She wanted to go to law school, she wanted to marry a doctor, and she wanted to have a child. And now at age 32 she had achieved all that, and found life unutterably boring and empty. The remarkable thing, however, in this case that readers may find amusing was that her view of surgery was that it was tantamount to butchery. She was terribly ashamed of the fact that her husband was a surgeon, and begged him in social circles not to identify himself as such but as a doctor, stating that people view the medical profession with a good deal of respect. So when people asked him what he does for a living, she'd like him to say he is a doctor, but not to admit being a surgeon. Her perception of a surgeon was tantamount to working in a delicatessen slicing roast beef. I asked the husband how he felt about this pejorative view that his wife had of his profession and he basically said, 'I think what I do is important, and I enjoy it, and if that's her view, that's her view. I am a doctor and I am a surgeon and I am not going to be pushed into feeling ashamed about my profession.' She launched a tremendous attack on him by saying that lawyers are people who have to use their brains, that it is a clean profession, one does not handle bodies and spilled guts and blood and gore, whereas what he does is purely mechanical and rote and requires minimal intelligence, and little more than manual dexterity. It was an amazing view that I had not heard expressed before.

Getting these people to diminish their fighting and clash points proved quite impossible. The husband seemed to be a mysogynist, who believed that women by nature are 'castrating, bitchy and demeaning' and there was no point in his even thinking about divorcing this woman and marrying somebody who admired and respected and loved him, because this is how women were. As he looked around at his friends and their marriages, theirs were no better than his. So he simply resigned to the fact that this was how it was and no one could change it. I found this incredibly frustrating. This couple did not derive any benefits, in spite of my most ardent efforts, so this is one recent case where I came away feeling less than fulfilled.

w.d.   What do you think of your own contribution to this case?

a.l.   Clearly I did not have whatever magic or vision, or the technology required to get this couple to do what would be best for them, whatever that might be. Should they divorce? Could they find a way around these barriers? I certainly failed, that why I am dwelling on this unusual couple. Surely the onus is partly on my shoulders for having failed to find the fulcrum and lever that might have shifted things for these people. I am hoping that they might consult someone else who will be able to do better by them.

w.d.   Is it your view that there is always such a fulcrum and lever, but it's just that we haven't found it yet? If so that's quite an optimistic view.

a.l.   Not always, but very often. Some individuals are really made from 'poor protoplasm', and we are not going to be able to do much here even if we find fulcrums and levers, because the substance itself is just too weak or unstable. But very often yes, I have what some people call the comic view of life, which carries a fairly high degree of optimism that many people who are not helped, could be helped if we knew more about what was going on.

w.d.   It was clear to you in this case, that you hadn't pressed the right set of buttons or pressed the right fulcrum or lever and unfortunately things didn't turn out too well.

A.L.   Correct. Maybe somebody else might have handled it differently. Perhaps if these people had gone to somebody who used paradoxical procedures, this might have been helpful – where the therapist might have used very heavy-handed paradoxes in accentuating and undermining what was going on thereby driving the couple closer, causing them to become more united against the common enemy, in this case the therapist. There are all kinds of possibilities and it is often a lot of fun, sitting around with colleagues bouncing around ideas such as this.

W.D.   Let's now consider a piece of work which left you feeling pleased.

A.L.   The piece of work that I was most pleased about over the past year is a man who had suffered a good deal, for many years. In fact I wrote him up in the epilogue of *The Practice of Multimodal Therapy* (Lazarus 1989). This man had been anxious and depressed and sorely beset by life since his mid-twenties. He was now in his sixties, having seen many, many therapists. He came to me after working at that time with a family systems therapist who was seeing this man, his wife, and adult son, and had written me a letter saying that this was a triadic, systemic collusional problem that required extensive family work, imploring me to be sure to bring in the entire family and to undermine the sabotaging that was going on. The therapist outlined a most involved, elaborate and intricate family system perspective. What struck me about this man was that he was extraordinarily timid and unassertive, that he was playing the role of a wimp, a doormat, a milksop. I decided to be really outspoken with this man and said to him, 'As long as you go through life playing that role I cannot see how you will feel other than you do. If I can persuade you to allow me to work with you on assertiveness skills you might begin to feel very different.' And that's what we did. I did not get into these elaborate adumbrations put forth by the family systems therapist; in fact I have never met this man's wife or son, but proceeded to work on direct targeted-focused-assertiveness-training with this man, who was a most able student and this turned his whole life around. The changes were quite remarkable. This is an interesting case, because there are times when one can go for a direct targeted response (rather than use a multimodal approach) that yields widespread ramifications and achieves a result that is quite startling. And so I was very happy about the outcome.

w.d.   But as far as I understand it, taking a multimodal view does not preclude taking a direct and focused approach to treatment on occasion.

a.l.   Correct. I am glad that this has come out because there are those who get the wrong impression and assume that I recommend that in every instance one must perform a thorough BASIC I.D. assessment and treatment. This is not necessary when something stands out like a beacon. I say, 'Do the most obvious thing first; don't look for trouble, trouble will find you. Do the most obvious thing first and if that doesn't work, then you can go back to the drawing board and do a much more thorough BASIC I.D. assessment or even a second order or a third order BASIC I.D. assessment or whatever seems necessary.'

w.d.   Changing tack somewhat, to what extent have you found the process of therapy, when you are in the role of therapist, therapeutic to you as a person?

a.l.   That's an interesting question, because I know that some therapists maintain that it needs to be a two-way street, that the therapist should grow from his or her patients. If you stop and consider that, I think it is rather absurd. If a therapist sees an average twenty or thirty clients a week and grows from each one, after ten years of practice, this therapist would have to be nothing less than a deity. It is true that one can learn something of value from almost anyone. I say this, by the way, because I have sometimes suggested to patients that they come into a group and they've objected, saying, 'Come on, what can I learn from neurotics like myself? If I am not talking to people with higher degrees and years of experience as therapists, this is a waste of my time.' And I point out to them that this is a most unfortunate view, because it is possible to learn from almost anyone. Consequently there is little doubt that in the course of meeting people clinically from time to time you may be told something by a patient that will inspire you, enlighten you, help you and it may be a two-way street at that moment.

w.d.   Can you think of some instances where that has happened to you?

a.l.   When I started out in clinical practice I was about 28 and I was treating some people in their forties and fifties who were certainly more worldly and experienced than I. These clients would adopt certain positions and tell me something drawn from their own lives which were far more extensive than mine at that time and I would come away learning something from a more experienced human being.

I remember, for instance, being profoundly influenced by an older man advising me never to put my work before my wife and children. I know that I must have acquired several bits of wisdom from clients over the years, but it's hard to be specific. So what I am saying is that sometimes you are going to learn something from your clients, but I think it's a mistake to look upon that as one of the primary purposes of therapy. The primary purpose is, of course, for you to help this suffering individual. I see it more as a one-way street.

w.d.   And do you find that as you accrued experience as a clinician over the years that these instances where you have benefited personally from the therapeutic process have diminished?

a.l.   The most accurate answer is that I simply don't know. Windy, many of these questions that you have raised are very pertinent, but these are issues I have not given a lot of thought to. I am giving you off-the-top responses. So let me think now whether of recent vintage I continue to receive as much from my clients as I did ten or twenty years ago. . . . I would be inclined to say, probably not, that it is more of a one-way street now than it was ten or twenty years ago, not because I have learned everything that there is to know, but certainly when you are let's say 28, and you are dealing with somebody who is 50, there is more of a chance that this experienced person can teach you a thing or two. But when you are 58, while you can certainly learn from somebody of 8 it is more likely that you will be doing 99 per cent of the teaching and instructing.

However, let me make one point about this area. There are some clinicians who think in terms of polarities, they say that good therapy should be a collaborative adventure, that this ought to be two people taking a journey together where patient and therapist will both come out enriched as opposed to the more austere view of a doctor treating a patient. I find it unfortunate that people think in these dichotomies and again would ask, when might one engage in a mutual soul-searching adventure in therapy and when might one elect not to do that but be the therapist treating the client? When would the treatment trajectory be one in which the therapist uses himself or herself as the major vehicle and when might it be more expedient for the therapist to rely more heavily on techniques, procedures and methods. As you know, Windy, I regard rigid rules (even the rigid rule never to have rigid rules) as counterproductive.

w.d.   You have given many workshops on multimodal therapy all over the USA and in other parts of the world, and presumably people in the audience have made critical comments about multimodal therapy. Which of these criticisms have you found most valid and a stimulus to the further development of your ideas?

A.L.   The criticisms, of course, vary according to the clinician's own experiences, background and prejudices. If I am talking to a predominantly psychodynamic audience, the criticisms are typically that my approach is far too active and that it is better to be more reflective and pensive. Again there is the problem – it's better to be one way as opposed to inquiring *when* is it better to be more pensive and reflective?

Some of the most important criticisms that have been levelled have been at the fact that it is so difficult to verify some of the main assumptions that I embrace. For example one of my main assumptions is that more is often better. The assumption here is that the more the person learns in therapy, the more coping skills the person acquires, the less likely this person will relapse. But how do you test that? How can one be more explicit about stating when certain methods do and do not apply? I think that the major criticisms have been directed at the fact that I am still talking at the level of generality, that my work has not achieved the degree of specificity that I would like to achieve. I would like to be able to say that under these and these particular conditions, this and this is most likely to apply, but we do not have the necessary knowledge yet for those prescriptions to be made. When I talk to behavioural audiences, they want more rigorous experimental backing, and more controlled research to support the points that I make, and all of these are valid criticisms.

Nevertheless, I think that most people have misunderstood what I am saying. I am saying that at this stage of our development in psychology in general, in social science across the board, we cannot afford to be unimodal, bimodal, trimodal, to hide behind one or two or three things that work well for us, and to apply them to all-comers. Technical eclecticism is the position that I am advocating. A technical eclectic looks everywhere that he or she can possibly look to find strategies that will prove useful and then applies them and tries to explain them as parsimoniously and as logically as possible. Perhaps if in my future workshops I dropped the term 'multimodal therapy' and spoke only of *technical eclecticism* and shared with the audience from a technically eclectic viewpoint the kinds of assessment procedures and therapeutic methods that seem to be most successful for specific problems, that might circumvent a lot of the criticisms that have been levelled to date. So I think that the criticisms have made me aware of the limitations of overstating the multimodal position and perhaps shifting to the broader technically eclectic posture.

w.d.   You mentioned research. Have there been many studies testing your hypothesis that when one takes a multimodal approach to assessment and treatment, then one will get more effective results?

a.l.   Yes, in Holland by Dr Maurits Kwee, who did some outcome research. Much of it is published in a book by Kwee and Roburgh (1987). There has been some work done in Scotland by Dr Thomas Williams (1988) in Glasgow, whose outcome study, comparing multimodal treatments with two others in treating children with learning disabilities, found the multimodal approach to be significantly superior. There have been other research endeavours trying to validate some of the techniques, trying to show inter-rater reliability and various validity indices for some of the tests and procedures that we have devised and these studies all seem to suggest that we are heading in the right direction. I cited numerous studies in the epilogue of my 1989 edition of *The Practice of Multimodal Therapy*.

w.d.   The term 'multi', which appears in the title of your works, is almost always attached to the word 'modal'. But the term 'multi' also appears in other people's descriptions of their work: I have seen articles on multi-factorial, multi-dimensional and multi-method approaches to therapy. What is your view of this work?

a.l.   The evolution of my own thinking, as already mentioned, started from a somewhat limited behavioural approach where I kept feeling that it was necessary to add more methods, ideas and techniques, and become more multi-faceted in what I was doing. This met with enormous opposition, but now I think most people are aware of the fact that human beings are multi-layered, multi-factored and multi-dimensional. As you point out, most people who are writing about effective treatment are 'multi' something. Many of these multi-dimensional, multi-factorial, multi-form or multi-method writings are very close to what I call 'multimodal', but few of them tend to acknowledge what I have done.

The other side, however, annoys me even more. A number of people write on multimodal therapy when they mean multi-dimensional, multi-method or multi-factorial. But there is no copyright on the term 'multimodal' and I have grown weary of writing to these people, pointing out that there are now about four or five dozen articles and more than half a dozen books on multimodal therapy. The difference between 'multimodal' and other 'multi-dimensional' approaches is that we spell out the BASIC I.D. and its derivatives and applications. It gets confusing when we use the same terms to mean different things. My protests don't get me very far, but I find it a little annoying when people use the term, which of course they are at liberty to do, in a very different way from my own, or in a very similar way to my own without any acknowledgement.

w.d.   Do you often find when you give workshops on your ideas that people come up to you and say 'You know I have been doing what you describe for years, I just don't call it multimodal therapy'?

a.l.   I have had people say, 'I just thought of myself as a good eclectic therapist and now that I have listened to what you have recommended, I realize that I am a multimodal therapist which I didn't know until today.' And I ask them whether they do in fact think in terms of BASIC I.D., employ methods like modality profiles that list the patient's problems across the BASIC I.D., obtain structural profiles that yield a quantitative rating of how people see themselves in each BASIC I.D. dimension, and so forth. Of course the answer to all of these questions is 'No'. So they do not use multimodal therapy as I define it, they do not employ strategies that we call 'bridging and tracking', which we don't have to go into here (see Lazarus 1989). I point out to these people that they might be good eclectic therapists but they are not multimodal unless they make use of some fairly specific assessment strategies that we have evolved.

w.d.   How many multimodal therapists are there in the world?

a.l.   In two words: 'not many'. It's interesting that there are some people in Holland, Germany and in Argentina who have been writing on the subject, applying it extensively and doing some research on multimodal methods. Most of the people who use it, however, are former students of mine. Some of my ex-students have obtained university positions and give courses in multimodal therapy. I also hear from certain sources that people whom I do not know have given courses in multimodal therapy at various American universities. I don't know what the numbers are, but certainly this does not equal the number of people who are enamoured of psychodynamic approaches or rational-emotive therapy or Beck's cognitive therapy.

w.d.   Are you concerned to promote multimodal therapy more?

a.l.   What I am concerned about promoting is a responsible integrationistic approach, a full understanding of technical eclecticism as opposed to theoretical eclecticism, and I am interested in disseminating ideas about the virtues of adopting a flexible, comprehensive, systematic position which we can call 'multimodal' or anything that seems more appropriate.

We need to look very carefully at the question that was raised by Gordon Paul and others; what therapy is most appropriate for this given individual and under which set of specific circumstances? I know that there are others who would argue against that and they talk about the need to develop more general helping processes that transcend individuals, but I find myself hard-pressed to see the value in that. I think that if one can come up with a wide range of well-documented treatments of choice that would enable one to say that this treatment should be used in this particular fashion with this kind of an individual when that kind of a process is happening, or when the patient is saying this, or looking that way, I think there will be far more hope of developing a truly effective treatment, and this is what I am looking towards.

w.d.   As you consider the future development of psychotherapy, do you think it will move in the direction of your own ideas on technical eclecticism?

a.l.   I think that Dr John Norcross has some data to suggest that technical eclecticism is a definite force, that many therapists regard science and research as something that they need to pay attention to. Yet there are large numbers of practising clinicians who view the field of scientific research with disdain and argue that the practice of psychotherapy is purely an art form, and that the disciplined light of science will elucidate nothing but small and irrelevant little building bricks. I think this is a most unfortunate view, but such thinkers are by no means a small minority. Many people elect to enter into the field and become therapists for their own personal religious reasons, and these people don't want you to confuse them with facts. If we can persuade more practitioners to give credibility to research and to understand what is coming out of the scientific laboratory, then in fact technical eclecticism and the ideas that I am espousing might very well become far more popular and widespread.

w.d.   Apart from the early part of your career your publications are almost exclusively clinical and theoretical. You are not noted for producing research publications. Would that be an accurate appraisal?

a.l.   I have worked in clinics and not in controlled laboratories. I look for strategies that are well researched, apply them clinically, and then talk about the exceptions that I find in my consulting room. I try to establish a two-way dialogue with the scientist in the laboratory. Thus I might say, 'It is all very well that you have found that using a technique like flooding is especially useful when dealing with certain kinds of anxiety disorders, but while implementing this strategy with clients, I had to develop an elaborate procedure to promote trust, obtain compliance, and augment it with relationship skills and other techniques.' I would then address this in a publication, so it would be an addendum to the sterile, you might say, finding in a laboratory being placed into the live dynamic flow of the consulting room and real life.

w.d.   So you see yourself as taking what researchers have found in their laboratories and testing the range of convenience of these findings in the clinic.

a.l.   That's very accurately put.

8

THE PERSONAL AND THE PROFESSIONAL

WINDY DRYDEN   In this final interview I would like to explore some personal factors with you as they impinge upon your work as a psychotherapist. Perhaps we could start off with your reflections concerning what drew you to this field?

ARNOLD LAZARUS   I think that most people are initially drawn to the field of psychotherapy for very personal reasons. They may find themselves in emotional hot water, undergo therapy, are able to resolve some of their own problems, and then may wish to use these insights to help others. Others may hope that by going into this field, they'll be helping themselves while helping others. Many people seem to be motivated by issues of that kind. My own deficits were shyness, feelings of inadequacy and hypersensitivity. Being the youngest family member, I was typically ignored and my opinion was considered unimportant. As I progressed in my studies of psychology my parents and siblings began to take note of what I was saying and by the time I had obtained a Masters degree they were more than somewhat respectful of my opinion. When I achieved my doctorate there was very much an aura of, you might say, fear that I had one over on them, that the knowledge that I had gained in becoming a psychologist had equipped me to be an assassin. I was then perceived as someone who had knowledge that could be used to heal or to help or that could be turned around and be used as a weapon in my own defence. The general message was, 'Don't mess with this fellow!' I am sure some of these selfish and personal factors played a role in my career choices.

W.D.   So what may have drawn you to the field in the first place were the deficits of shyness and not being taken seriously. But it seemed to you that the more you progressed in the field, the more you were taken seriously. Did that serve to reinforce your interest?

A.L.   Yes. In addition to my three siblings, I had many, many uncles, aunts and cousins (I might mention that all my aunts and uncles have since died). Because I was by far the youngest this extended family group played an important role throughout my childhood, adolescence and early adulthood and these were the people who tended to regard me as the young kid. Certain uncles, aunts and older cousins were very significant throughout the first twenty-five to thirty years of my life. Many of them bullied me, poked fun at me, and put me down. When they began to sit up and take notice, this became very important to me personally and undoubtedly had a profound influence. That's the negative motivation. The positive motivation, in retrospect, was that when I was about 15 or 16 many of my peers turned to me for help and support: they told me that I was easy to talk to, that I was understanding and useful to them. I might say that I was under the impression that in order to practise psychotherapy you had to be a physician, a medically trained individual, and I was never interested in going through a formal medical education. The idea of attending medical school and spending hours poring over anatomy and physiology and biochemistry books had zero appeal. And so I went into entirely different avenues. In fact I started university with a view to becoming a journalist, a writer, and it was only when I discovered that one could indeed pursue a career in psychotherapy without a medical degree, that I became really interested in psychology and psychotherapy.

w.d.   Did you follow any family tradition by entering the field of psychology and psychotherapy?

a.l.   Basically no. I have always been a trail-blazer. In fact no one in my immediate family even went to college, and only a small number of my cousins became professionals. The majority went into small businesses. My father was in a small retail business, as were my grandparents, my brother, my brother-in-law and virtually all of my uncles. I had more than ten uncles who operated small retail businesses.

w.d.   In which approaches to therapy were you initially trained?

a.l.   In Rogerian and psychodynamic traditions predominantly.

w.d.   Did you resonate with these approaches?

a.l.   Initially I was enchanted. I had found the psychoanalytic ideas to be compelling. They provided me with the false notion of having X-ray vision, making me feel that from the smallest samples of behaviour I could infer the most poignant realities about people. I remember when I was engaged to be married and my mother-in-law, who was extremely house-proud, was running her fingers along a cupboard to see if there was any dust. I recall turning to my fiancée at the time and saying, 'Do you know what your mother is *really* doing?' and went on to explain the anal-retentive obsessive-compulsive underpinnings of her behaviour and its entire Oedipal, pre-Oedipal and developmental implications. You see, I think there is this false feeling of possessing a sort of psychic X-ray machine that compels the psychodynamic people to continue in this vein. So there was an enormous appeal and the entire process of trying to understand the dynamics and discussing these factors was also extremely interesting. The Rogerian backup at the time gave one an immediate entry into therapy. The notion was that you were unlikely to do much harm by remaining reflective, pensive and empathic and so it was all right to begin to practise in some way. I became disenchanted when I began to see that worthwhile results were not forthcoming. Initially I feared that I had entered the wrong field, that other people using these methods would achieve rapid remissions in their clients, while I just didn't have the talent. I then looked carefully at my senior trainers and professors and obtained information on some of their outcomes, and saw that they were also not getting spectacular results, to put it mildly. This is when I began to seek something different, something that would rest on an empathic, caring, considerate and respectful base, but offer very much more.

w.d.   How did you become interested in behaviour therapy?

a.l.   Around 1956 there were a number of people associated with the university where I was training, who called themselves 'conditioning therapists' and they had become interested in using a variety of methods with patients. One of them was Joseph Wolpe who was doing one-way mirror work, and for the first time I sat and observed somebody doing role-playing and assertiveness training, relaxation and desensitization. My initial response was one of great scepticism because here was somebody violating all the cardinal rules that I had been taught to observe: the rules of maintaining distance and not intervening actively and not being directive. Yet I sat behind the mirror week after week and observed what he and others were doing. I would see undeniable improvements and this together with some encouragement from a few fellow students who were interested in this orientation led me to experiment myself with these methods. It was quite amazing to me when upon adopting a more directive stance I began to find that indeed people were making gains, were deriving benefits, although I was warned subsequently by my mainstream teachers that these gains would be

short-lived, if not deleterious in the long run. It was not easy for me
to embrace a more active behavioural viewpoint. It was not an
overnight thing.

w.d.   What was the nature of that struggle?

a.l.   The nature of the struggle was trying to determine who was
right. Was it true that if you didn't delve into the underpinnings,
the dynamics, that you would find people ending up in mental
hospitals because of malignant symptom substitution? Was it true
that treating what they called 'symptoms' was like giving somebody
complaining of stomach pains a shot of morphine and then pop
goes the appendix and the person dies of peritonitis? These were
the kinds of medical analogies that were always used. Was there
some truth to this? How could I, at that stage, as a young fledgling
student, argue against the experience and knowledge of people
many years my senior? And at the same time, the lunatic fringe as
they called these conditioning therapists whom I subsequently
christened 'behaviour therapists', really seemed to be helping many
people. They were regarded as irresponsible, poorly trained and
dangerous. In fact our meetings used to take place in a clandestine
setting, for I was afraid that if my formal or official trainers knew
that I was associating with these people I would be expelled from
my internship. I could get into serious trouble and this was not a
paranoid delusion. There was a lot of truth to this. And in fact most
of us who participated in these evening cabals tended to be very
circumspect about what we were doing. That was the essence of the
struggle.

w.d.   How did you resolve that struggle?

a.l.   I resolved that struggle over a period of years, by noting that the
dire consequences that were predicted did not ensue; that, people
whom I had treated behaviourally did not end up by necessarily
relapsing and developing new symptoms. I also resolved the
struggle by pinning these critics down and asking them to give me a
prediction as to how long it would take before we would notice the
negative impact of what they considered superficial, mechanistic
ideas and procedures. I began to find that when I asked them to be
more specific, for example 'Will the person end up in a hospital in
three months, or will it take longer than that?', I would get evasive
answers. I then remembered that when I was a young boy in
religious training and would ask any clergyman certain questions, I
would be told those questions are not to be asked, they are beyond
the pale. When I began to get similar answers from my psychotherapy trainers, I came to realize that these people had a religious

belief in what they were doing and it was like talking to a priest or a rabbi rather than to a scientist. By this time, I had become convinced that if we didn't follow the rigorous scientific method in psychotherapy, we would forever more simply be collectors of anecdotes, rather than purveyors of knowledge. This certainly helped to disabuse me of the notion that the mainstream establishment of psychiatrists, psychologists, professors and trainers were the ones I should follow.

w.d.   Was it at this point that Joseph Wolpe became your mentor?

a.l.   That's correct: it was round about 1956 that I felt terribly proud to become a para-professional, helping him with one woman who was agoraphobic, taking her on *in vivo* driving excursions, walking excursions and generally helping with the relaxation training. I felt very, very proud that I was allowed to do this. I noted the improvements in this woman. I sat behind the one-way mirror and I saw assertiveness training and desensitization methods being used to good effect. I might add, by the way, that this woman had been scheduled to have a pre-frontal lobotomy, because three psychiatrists considered her anxiety and agoraphobic avoidance intractable. The treatment of this particular case was a pivotal turning-point in my career.

w.d.   How long did your working relationship with Wolpe last?

a.l.   Well, it lasted pretty much until 1959, when Wolpe was the chair of my PhD dissertation. He had gone to Stanford, California, for a year around 1957 and returned to South Africa in 1958 and then I think emigrated in 1960, when he was given a position at the University of Virginia in Charlottesville, Virginia, at the medical school. We continued to correspond and I visited him in 1963 and he visited South Africa once or twice and then in 1967 I became a full professor at Temple University Medical School where Wolpe had been appointed full professor the previous year. We had adjoining offices for three and a half years in Philadelphia.

w.d.   At what point did that relationship end?

a.l.   It ended pretty much a year or so later, around 1968. The details and the dynamics of that situation are not worth going into here, but the basic clash points were around several clinical issues. My sense was that what he was doing was too narrow and I recommended ways and means in which behaviour therapy procedures, techniques and methods and theories could be expanded, and Wolpe saw these ideas as quite heretical and antithetical to what he was doing. A good deal of acrimony arose as a result, and so I left Temple University Medical School in 1970 and became visiting professor and director of clinical training at Yale in 1970.

w.d.   Did the breakdown in that relationship serve to stimulate your thinking and encourage your independence of thought or did you take some time to regroup after that?

a.l.   I found the entire thing exceedingly distressing, but I immediately started writing and lecturing on my ideas. In 1971 my book called *Behavior Therapy and Beyond* was published (Lazarus 1971). Many people regard it as one of the very first books on cognitive-behaviour therapy, because in that book for the first time, I emphasized the value of cognition in addition to behaviour. This was not well received by mainstream behaviour therapists. People like Hans Eysenck at the University of London as well as Wolpe and his followers were extraordinarily unimpressed with this 'mentalistic addition'. I was pretty much defrocked or expelled from the behaviour therapy camp as it existed in those days, despite the fact that I won the election as president of the Association for Advancement of Behavior Therapy. I might add that Wolpe had written to the entire membership urging them to elect Leonard Ullmann as president, but I won the election. We will never know whether it was because of or in spite of Wolpe's propaganda against me. But that gives you a flavour of some of the tension that existed, and how these innovations were not viewed with much favour by the committed behaviour therapy crowd.

w.d.   What was the response to your new ideas?

a.l.   As you could predict, there was a bifurcation. I had a coterie of supporters who were very much in favour of what I was doing and I had those detractors who felt that my approach was entirely vacuous. As soon as you take a stand on any issue you acquire supporters and detractors.

w.d.   What stimulated the development of your ideas as expressed in the book *Behavior Therapy and Beyond* five years later to those in your first book on *Multimodal Behavior Therapy* as it was called then (Lazarus 1976)?

a.l.   *Behavior Therapy and Beyond* stated that we needed to add many more techniques and several additional ideas to the ones that the dyed-in-the-wool behaviour therapists were employing. It espoused various methods and procedures that were not used by most members of the Association for the Advancement of Behavior Therapy at the time. Subsequently I saw that we needed to go beyond that and add still more techniques but also to find a systematic framework, a template that would guide the practitioner. If two aspirins are good for you ten aspirins are not five times better: there is a point of diminishing returns and it was clear that one could not simply become a technique collector. You have to place these techniques within the parameters of a systematic framework and this is why the multimodal notions were developed. While searching for that particular framework, I asked 'What do we study as psychologists? Don't we study the way people behave and feel, don't we study sensations and images and thoughts and relationships? Is this not the essence of what psychology is comprised of? If the answer is in the affirmative can we afford to neglect any of these modalities in our clinical endeavours, in our diagnoses, in our assessments, in our problem identification procedures?' These were the questions that were posed in search of a far more systematic comprehensive interactive framework.

w.d.   Did the fact that you called your first book on multimodal therapy *Multimodal Behavior Therapy* (Lazarus 1976) indicate a reluctance to let go of the behaviour therapy affiliation?

a.l.   Yes, I began to see what I was doing as a more forward-looking advanced behaviour therapy. Calling the book *Multimodal Behavior Therapy* was intended to separate it from other traditional forms of behaviour therapy – this was supposed to underscore greater breadth. Subsequently it occurred to me that what I was advocating was multimodal behavioural therapy, multimodal cognitive therapy, multimodal imagery therapy and so forth across the BASIC I.D. and that the emphasis was not on any one modality. So to call it multimodal behaviour therapy was misleading. Thus, I dropped the 'behaviour' and it became 'multimodal therapy', which (as you and I have discussed previously) might be a misnomer. It might have been better to have called it 'multimodal assessment and comprehensive psychotherapy' or something like that.

w.d.   What were the personal satisfactions and the personal costs that you experienced in your development from behaviour therapist to multimodal therapist?

a.l.   The major satisfactions arose from having a compass that could guide me through the maze when I ran into clinical difficulties. I would draw on the BASIC I.D. and would find to my own delight that very often answers were forthcoming. Students and colleagues who tried this also independently verified the same impressions. Fledgling novices, beginning students, would report that thanks to this framework, they felt more confident when confronted by some of their first clinical cases. They knew how to ask pertinent questions and how to zoom in on significant areas instead of being bewildered by the mass of stimuli that descended upon them. They thanked me for providing them with this lodestar, this guidepost. Those were some of the major satisfactions. The dissatisfactions stemmed from the fact that the purely scientifically minded people failed to see the value in what I was doing, but were openly critical of the fact that there was little empirical research behind what was being offered. And they would tend to throw the proverbial baby out with the bath-water by completely denigrating the entire approach.

There is an interesting fact about the field of behaviour therapy. Many of the leading figures are themselves not therapists. For example Hans Eysenck, who has been a leading spokesperson for behaviour therapy, has never treated a patient in his life. There is an enormous difference in my opinion between academics or pure researchers who sit in ivory towers or in sealed laboratories, versus those of us who are in the trenches, you might say, dealing with the battlefront conditions of patient care and responsibility. The naivety of the academicians and pure researchers never ceases to amaze me. What was also interesting was that many a researcher who then began clinical practice was humbled within a year or two and began to talk far differently from their stereotypic rigid ways when they were pure researchers. But many figures in the behavioural arena are not clinicians, not therapists. Apart from Eysenck, Albert Bandura, one of the very biggest names in behavioural circles, is not a therapist; Leonard Krasner has done very limited clinical practice. Most of these people, as I keep saying, were predominantly scholars, writers and researchers. Another name that is very prominent in the behaviour therapy literature is Cyril Franks, who is a colleague of mine. Cyril Franks is not a therapist. People with very limited clinical experience or with none whatsoever were the most strident critics of my work. Now these are the people who have the most power, because they write. Perhaps in Vienna when Freud was practising there were people who were far more brilliant than him, but they didn't write, so we never heard about them. Perhaps they did wondrous things with their patients but only those people who publish are the ones who are heard of and well known. On the other hand it was gratifying to receive letters from practitioners who thanked me for my efforts and claimed to find multimodal therapy very valuable. But as I said, most of my critics did not attack me in personal letters but in published articles, reviews and comments.

w.d.   What was your personal response to these criticisms?

A.L.   My personal response to these criticisms was a feeling of overwhelming frustration. I often felt that these people did not know what they were talking about, because they had not encountered the difficulties and problems that clinicians face, that what they believed was just too pat: it didn't work that way in the real world. I would challenge or simply invite these people to try for themselves to do what they consider so simple and textbook-like, and see how seldom it works: that treatment adherence and a wide range of positive outcomes calls for personal skills that are not so easily achieved as their theories assume.

W.D.   That brings us to the publication in 1981 of your major text, which has just been reprinted with an update chapter in 1989 (Lazarus 1981; 1989). How has multimodal therapy developed since 1981?

A.L.   In the epilogue in the 1989 edition I mentioned a fair amount of research that has been done since 1981. A number of students have written dissertations testing out aspects of the multimodal approach, and several professional journals have devoted entire issues to the use of the BASIC I.D. There are reports in which multimodal methods were applied to career counselling, used in rehabilitation settings, in crisis intervention, thus showing its utility beyond the confines of the consulting room. Some new assessment instruments have been developed and factor analytic studies and validity studies have borne out quite a number of our clinical observations. So since 1981 there has been continued interest in multimodal notions as well as some growth and refinement. We added some new concepts that we think are important in understanding people that had not come to our attention in 1981 and these are all mentioned in the epilogue. I think it's fair to say that there has been a steady refinement and growth in multimodal methods.

W.D.   Your own ideas changed quite radically from 1966 when your first book with Joseph Wolpe was published until 1981. Has that degree of radicalism been present from 1981 to date?

A.L.   No. The extensive changes and additions and refinements that were made between 1966 and 1981 show much more of a plateau during the past ten years. But don't forget that as a technical eclectic I am constantly looking for others to give me new ideas, better methods, and so forth. I don't find that I am the one who has to be the innovator. Quite frankly there do not seem to be many wonderful things happening right now. As I see it, across the board, there seems to be a plateau in the applied clinical area. I am hoping that soon there is going to be some sort of breakthrough worthy of the name from some source, and I hope to get that information.

w.d.   You have been a therapist now for about thirty-four years. Have you always managed to sustain your enthusiasm for the field or have there been periods where you have become less enthusiastic or indeed unenthusiastic?

a.l.   I guess that is most easily answered by a simple anecdote. A number of us were sitting around discussing the familiar question that so many people ask, namely how would our lives change if we came into a lot of money. Some people said they would do exactly what they are now doing, which means either they are very fortunate, or they lack imagination. I said that if I came into a lot of money I would probably try my hand at something entirely different. I might try writing television scripts, I might try and write novels or plays, and since I had a lot of money, it wouldn't matter if I succeeded, it would be done for the sheer enjoyment. But notice what I am saying, I would in fact be trying out a different career, I would probably still keep my clinical hand in and work with a few fascinating clients, but on the whole, I doubt if I would continue being an active professor, training, doing therapy, giving lectures, writing books, or talking to Windy Dryden about matters such as this. If I had a lot of money, rather than do what we are now doing, I would invite you on to my yacht so that we would take a little cruise, have dinner in a fabulous restaurant and go on to a wonderful play. So maybe that answers the question you posed.

w.d.   We spoke in our earlier interview of how important it is for human beings to have fun, to be fulfilled and to enjoy themselves. It sounds as if some of the fun and enjoyment has gone out of the work for you at present.

a.l.   That's neither entirely true, nor entirely untrue. I still experience a good deal of pleasure although as I said before, I don't think that we are in the field for our own edification and pleasure, although some therapists seem to think that we should be. I know that many people in our field say that doing therapy is or should be fun. In the earlier interview I mentioned to you that this view has always struck me as self-indulgent. At times it can be fun, but if properly done, it is *jolly hard work*. Sure there are peak experiences, high moments and points of joy. The longer you do it the less 'fun' it becomes. I think that this is inevitable. I think that for most people, a certain habituation sets in; it's like romance, you know, it's not an endless process. You meet the person of your dreams, fall in love and marry, but thirty-four years later you don't feel exactly as you did on your honeymoon. So any therapist who claims to be as ardently enthusiastic about his or her work forty-plus years later would be quite an anomaly.

w.d.   If you had your time again, without the advantages of the large financial windfall, would you still have entered the field and if so, is there anything you might have done differently in your career up to this date?

a.l.   If you are asking whether I could go back in time, knowing what I now know, and relive my life, and whether I would select a different career, it would depend on whether or not I am the same Arnold Lazarus. In other words, if I am essentially the same person except that I possess additional information, the changes would not be enormous because I would still have the same limitations. With my present limitations I could never be a brilliant brain surgeon, or a concert pianist, or a fabulous athlete. So there's no other profession that I would or could choose that would prove more rewarding. But let's say I could be anything I wanted to be and whatever inherent limitations I have would be removed. Do you know what I would choose, under those conditions? I would choose to do what Steven Spielberg does. I would choose to be a writer, a director working in the film industry, having the enormous fun of creation that these individuals have. So if I could be anything I wanted to, I would definitely not choose to be a psychotherapist. But if I am Arnold Lazarus, who could never be a Spielberg, then I would do just what I have done. I would choose psychology and psychotherapy, evolve and develop multimodal therapy and do the same thing all over again.

w.d.   As I was turning the tape over you remarked that your sense of humour was missing from these interviews. Do you have any thoughts on why that should be so?

a.l.   Yes, what I was saying to you, is that many people have emphasized that one of the most outstanding features of the way I operate professionally and personally is that I employ a good deal of *humour*. I am often able to get clients to laugh good-naturedly at themselves. I don't think that any of this has come across in these interviews. I think I have been trying to underscore what I regard as some of the serious issues in this field. So let me mention, in passing, that there is a definite place in my work for humour and levity. Now back to serious issues!

w.d.   In an interview that I conducted with Albert Ellis (Dryden 1989) he discussed the place of his work in psychotherapy in the context of the rest of his life. He said that in his life, his work came first, he came second, because he gave up other pleasures for work, and the woman in his life came third. Now if you were to place your work as a therapist and as a writer of books on psychotherapy into the overall context of your life, how would you place it?

A.L.   I have frequently made the observation that what sets me apart from most of my colleagues is that they seem to live for their work, whereas I work in order to live. My wife and kids have always come first, followed by the cultivation of really meaningful friendships and the pursuit of fun (plays, movies, tennis, country walks, music, restaurants, travel and social gatherings).

W.D.   And what about your work?

A.L.   Let me restate the hierarchy: I would put my wife and children first, time spent with close friends and other family members would then be next, and my work (meaning intellectual stimulation, social contributions and economic survival) would come in third place.

W.D.   How would you sum up your contribution to the field of psychotherapy to date?

A.L.   First, let me ask if I have made a contribution. It's very hard to know whether one's ideas have significant merit. The world has not beaten a path to my door. From time to time, I receive letters and calls from people here and abroad telling me about something I had written that they had found useful personally or professionally. So I do get my reinforcements. But to answer your question differently, remembering that I started out from a psychodynamic and Rogerian standpoint and then rejected their methods as *weak*, I'd like to think that I helped to promote the use of more powerful procedures in their place. If I have made a contribution, it is that I first showed that behaviour therapy can be truly humanistic (c.f. my 1971 book *Behavior Therapy and Beyond*), then I broadened its horizons by emphasizing the importance of cognitions (following Ellis), and finally I developed an even broader and more systematic framework in my writings on multimodal methods. While observing other therapists, I became more and more aware that they were not doing enough. I would see others' clients who had benefited from their treatments, but I would be surprised that in the course of their therapy many obvious problems had not been addressed. For example they were not provided with certain interpersonal skills that could easily be learned. Now of course they were not taught various skills because they'd gone to therapists who didn't do that, who only provided a caring relationship, or who only believed in the exploration of childhood encounters. Too bad. It seems to be a matter of luck for clients to find their way to a therapist who can give them what they need. I have endeavoured to contribute, in a systematic way, more and more breadth to the field. Many people are now espousing similar views. Narrowness seems to be fading from many quarters and whereas ten, fifteen or twenty years ago I was viewed as an iconoclast for promoting these notions of *breadth* rather than *depth* (there is still such a fondness for people to talk about how deep an issue is, whereas I would argue that it is clinically far more expedient to determine how broadly based it is, how different facets are involved). The depth phenomenon I think has retarded effective strategies from being implemented. So my contribution is tied to the fact that I have tried to be systematic and very comprehensive, and to supply an exhaustive range of strategies for assessing significant interactions across many modalities.

w.d.   How do you feel when you consider the future of your work in the field?

a.l.   I said earlier that my nuclear family comes before my work, and this emphasis has now resulted in an unexpected turn of events. My son, Clifford, who had considered a medical career, changed his mind and completed a PhD in Clinical Psychology. He is young, eager and raring to go, and I find myself thoroughly enjoying his enthusiasm and hope to collaborate with him on projects. We have already made a number of revisions to the multimodal question-naire that we use, developed the Structural Profile Inventory and have co-authored a few chapters. Cliff is talking about the possibility of founding a training centre, and being far more entrepreneurial about this entire endeavour than I have been. He also has some different ideas and is involved in extensive research projects and so there is a new-found enthusiasm in putting my son's career before my own. I am very eager to give him a good start, and find myself deriving infinitely more pleasure from helping his ideas grow than from reiterating my own.

w.d.   So one Lazarus is resurrecting the other Lazarus's enthusiasm.

a.l.   Quite so. But in terms of my present interests, they lie in examining the values and limitations of different forms of psycho-therapy integration.

FURTHER READING

For those who wish to read further about the work of Arnold Lazarus, the following books and articles are suggested.

Lazarus, A. A. (1988) A multimodal perspective on problems of sexual desire, in S. R. Leiblum and R. C. Rosen (eds) *Sexual Desire Disorders*, New York: Guilford. This chapter provides a good illustration of how the multimodal therapy approach is employed when treating a focal area of disturbance.

Lazarus, A. A. (1989) *The Practice of Multimodal Therapy*, Baltimore, Md: Johns Hopkins University Press. This is an updated edition of the original 1981 work. It is the most comprehensive statement of Lazarus's position on the multimodal approach to therapy and can be viewed as a standard work.

Lazarus, A. A. (1989) Multimodal therapy, in R. J. Corsini and D. Wedding (eds) *Current Psychotherapies*, 4th edn, Itasca, Ill: Peacock. This chapter is an excellent summary of the overall multimodal position. It affords the reader the opportunity to compare and contrast multimodal therapy with more than a dozen other approaches.

Lazarus, A. A. (1989) Why I am an eclectic (not an integrationist), *British Journal of Guidance and Counselling* 17: 248–58. The pitfalls of trying to combine different theories are emphasized, and instead, the virtues of selecting effective techniques from different disciplines, while remaining theoretically constant, are spelled out.

Lazarus, A. A. (1990) Can psychotherapists transcend the shackles of their training and superstitions?, *Journal of Clinical Psychology* 46: 351–8. This paper criticizes many aspects of formal training in psychotherapy, underscores errors that many supervisors commit, and offers several constructive remedies to ensure that therapists get the sort of training that will render them truly effective with their clients.

Lazarus, A. A. and Lazarus, C. N. (1990) Emotions: a multimodal therapy perspective, in R. Plutchik and H. Kellerman (eds) *Emotion: Theory, Research and Experience, Vol. 5*: Emotion, Psychopathology and Psychotherapy, San Diego, Calif: Academic Press. The multimodal understanding of emotion is clearly articulated in this chapter. Details are provided of

the ways in which affect interacts with behaviour, sensations, images, cognitions, interpersonal processes and biological factors.
Lazarus, A. A. and Mayne, T. J. (1990) Relaxation: some limitations, side effects, and proposed solutions, *Psychotherapy* 27: 261–6. Underscoring the emphasis on specificity that characterizes multimodal assessment and therapy, this article spells out various negative effects that relaxation techniques can have and ways of overcoming them.

REFERENCES

Barlow, D. H. (1988) *Anxiety and its Disorders: The Nature and Treatment of Anxiety and Panic*, New York: Guilford.

Bernard, M. E. and DiGiuseppe, R. (eds) (1989) *Inside Rational-Emotive Therapy*, San Diego, Calif: Academic Press.

Corsini, R. J. and Wedding, D. (eds) (1989) *Current Psychotherapies*, 4th edn, Itasca, Ill: Peacock.

Dryden, W. (1986) Eclectic psychotherapies: a critique of leading approaches, in J. C. Norcross (ed.) *Handbook of Eclectic Psychotherapy*, New York: Brunner/Mazel.

Dryden, W. (1987) Theoretically consistent electicism: humanizing a computer 'addict', in J. C. Norcross (ed.) *Casebook of Eclectic Psychotherapy*, New York: Brunner/Mazel.

Dryden, W. (1989) Albert Ellis: an efficient and passionate life, *Journal of Counseling and Development* 67: 539–46.

Ellis, A. and Yeager, R. J. (1989) *Why Some Therapies don't Work: The Dangers of Transpersonal Psychology*, Buffalo, NY: Prometheus.

Howard, G. S., Nance, D. W. and Myers, P. (1987) *Adaptive Counseling and Therapy*, San Francisco, Calif: Jossey-Bass.

Kwee, M. G. T. and Roburgh, M. R. H. M. (1987) *Multimodale Therapie: Praktijk, Theorie En Onderzoek*, Lisse (Holland): Swets & Zeitlinger.

Lazarus, A. A. (1971) *Behavior Therapy and Beyond*, New York: McGraw-Hill.

Lazarus, A. A. (1976) *Multimodal Behavior Therapy*, New York: Springer.

Lazarus, A. A. (1977) Toward an egoless state of being, in A. Ellis and R. Grieger (eds) *Handbook of Rational-Emotive Therapy*, New York: Springer.

Lazarus, A. A. (1981) *The Practice of Multimodal Therapy*, New York: McGraw-Hill.

Lazarus, A. A. (1989) *The Practice of Multimodal Therapy*, Baltimore, Md: Johns Hopkins University Press (updated paperback edn).

Mullen, P. E. (1989) Psychoanalysis: a creed in decline, *Australian and New Zealand Journal of Psychiatry* 23: 17–20.

Prochaska, J. O. and DiClemente, C. C. (1986) The transtheoretical approach, in J. C. Norcross (ed.) *Handbook of Eclectic Psychotherapy*, New York: Brunner/Mazel.

Shapiro, D. A. and Shapiro, D. (1983) Comparative therapy outcome research: methodological implications of meta-analysis, *Journal of Consulting and Clinical Psychology* 51: 42–53.

Smith, M. L., Glass, G. V. and Miller, T. I. (1980) *The Benefits of Psychotherapy*, Baltimore, Md: Johns Hopkins University Press.

Wedding, D. and Corsini, R. J. (eds) *Case Studies in Psychotherapy*, Itasca, Ill.: Peacock.

Williams, T. (1988) A multimodal approach to assessment and intervention with children with learning disabilities, unpublished doctoral dissertation, Department of Psychology, University of Glasgow.

INDEX